christian family
guide to

Family Activities

Series Editor: James S. Bell Jr.

by Marilee LeBon and
Amy Wall with
Janet Lee

ALPHA

A member of Penguin Group (USA) Inc.

International Standard Book Number: 1-59257-077-1
Library of Congress Catalog Card Number: 2003104304

05   04   03   8   7   6   5   4   3   2   1

Interpretation of the printing code: The rightmost number of the first series of numbers is the year of the book's printing; the rightmost number of the second series of numbers is the number of the book's printing. For example, a printing code of 03-1 shows that the first printing occurred in 2003.

Printed in the United States of America

Contents

Appendixes

Introduction

It seems like just last summer that I discovered my preschool-aged girls painting our Springer Spaniel with watercolors in our backyard. But that was 10 years ago. Today Megan is in middle school and Elizabeth is a freshman in high school, and I can't even get them to *walk* the dog! Our time with our families is so short! It's important that we make the most of our time together. We need to laugh and play together and celebrate the incredible creative bent that God has given each of his children, however uniquely it is expressed. And we need to bind our children to us with traditions and memories that will last long after they leave our homes.

Like so many families today, I understand the many pressures of time and finances that seem to work against our best efforts to spend quality time with our families. Work, school, and even the church make claims on our evenings and weekends—time when we should be building strong family ties. Add to that the growing influence of the media, the Internet, and their peers, and it is quite possible to go days without meaningful communication between family members.

We need to start enjoying our families more! That's what this book is about—it provides practical and inspiring ways to play together as a family. It gives creative ideas for crafts and holiday traditions and how-to's for party-planning to celebrate those special moments in your family life. With everything from game rules to craft tips and recipes, we trust that this book will become a ready reference for you as you create lasting family memories.

What's in This Book

In this book you will find great ideas for playing together and building family traditions and memories. This book is organized into the following three parts:

Part 1, "The Family That Plays Together Stays Together!" contains a collection of games—both new and classic—that you can use to plan family activity night for hours and hours of fun and laughter. We give many rules of play, variations of standard games, and ideas for family gatherings, along with advice on how to make time in your family to play together.

Holiday traditions are key to building lasting family memories. In **Part 2, "Holiday Happenings,"** you will find great home-decorating ideas, gift ideas to make and share, recipes from the kitchen, and simple crafts that can involve every member of your family in creating a festive atmosphere in your home in every season.

There are great memory-making opportunities for families when they come together to celebrate special people and occasions—from birthdays to graduations to anniversaries! In **Part 3, "Parties and Get-Togethers,"** you will find all kinds of practical ways to plan the perfect gatherings for family and friends and unique ways to preserve those family memories.

Bonus Bits of Information

If you thumb through this book, you'll find interesting sidebars with tidbits of information, inspirational quotes and Scripture, definitions of important terms, and tips for strengthening your family ties.

That's the Spirit

These boxes contain quotes and Scripture verses to inspire you and put family activities into a Christ-centered context, and biblical truths to share with your family about values that are important to you as well as blessings for special family occasions.

Plain and Simple

def·i·ni·tion

In these boxes you'll find definitions of key terms about games and crafts along with additional information on holidays and get-togethers. Look for terms like **anagram**—a word or phrase created by transposing the letters in another word or phrase.

Family Ties

Family Ties boxes hold words of encouragement to help you build that team spirit in your family and learn to enjoy each other more. How to encourage cooperation and participation are just some of the timely tips you'll find.

Guess What?

Here you'll find trivia and additional bits of information about games, holidays, and other activities for your family. You'll find out about the origins of many classic games and the meaning of traditional holiday symbols like Easter eggs and Christmas stars.

Part 1

The Family That Plays Together Stays Together!

It takes both love and laughter to make a happy home. You can add more of both of these essential ingredients to your family relationships by setting aside time for your family to play together. You can make the most of the time and opportunities you have by following some of the simple guidelines in the following chapters.

Playing games together strengthens your family ties in many ways. Spending time together encourages your family to communicate. Games teach teamwork and cooperation—essential components in the life of a healthy family. Games also teach important values like fair play, honesty, and how to both win and lose graciously. The information in the following chapters provides you with a great resource for planning family activity nights, parties, and other playtimes together. They also provide you with instructions on how to play some of your favorite games from your own childhood and introduce you and your children to new games.

Chapter 1

Learning to Play Together

Technology is wonderful and we can be thankful for the freedom, fun, and health technology brings to us. It takes less time to do the laundry today than it did even a generation ago. But instead of using the time we've gained to love and enjoy our families more, we've rushed to fill the time with activities that often isolate us even more from one another. So before we grow too nostalgic or raise the battle cry for an anti-technology society, we should remember that the fault doesn't lie in technology, but rather in ourselves.

Think about a typical day in the life of your family. If your family is anything like mine, your days are spent at different locations—school for the kids, work or home for Mom and Dad—only to come together in the evening for a few minutes of actual "together" time. Then everyone is off again to church committee meetings, soccer practice, piano lessons, and on it goes. On those rare evenings when you are all actually in the same house together, you'll find Sarah is in her room talking to her girlfriend on the telephone, Josh is on the computer doing research for a school report, Dad is trying to finish that project you've been nagging him about in the garage, and Mom is trying to get baby Megan ready for bed.

It's pretty obvious that if we want to have a family that plays together, we need to make the time for play. We can't just add more to our already crowded schedules—something will have to go. But whatever it is that as parents you decide to forego in order to spend playtime with your children, you can be sure that God will multiply tenfold the benefits in the quality of your family relationships.

That's the Spirit

Jesus understands about the busyness of your life. Even in his time, life could become so hectic that there was no time to draw close to those most important to you.

Then Jesus said, "Let's get away from the crowds for a while and rest." There were so many people coming and going that Jesus and his apostles didn't even have time to eat. (Mark 6:31)

Finding the Time to Play

We'd like to think that life was simpler a hundred or a thousand years ago. It would ease our conscience if we could say they had more time for play "back then." But the truth is, we have exactly the same number of hours in a day that they did and fewer of them are consumed with pure survival. So if they found time to play, we certainly can! Here are some tips on how to find more time to play with your family:

- **Be spontaneous.** With children, playful moments just happen. Someone tosses a pillow a little too hard, and you can have either a brawl or a game. Your three-year-old launches into a silly song in the middle of aisle 5 of the grocery store. You can chide her for singing at the top of her lungs and "disturbing" others, or you can join in the fun. Make a game of it—one of you sings the beginning of a phrase and the other must sing the ending.

Guess What?

Archaeologists have discovered a Babylonian board game, dated around 4000 B.C., that resembles our Chess and Checkers. In ancient Sumeria (3000 B.C.), they played a game similar to Backgammon. Playing cards were first used in Asia around A.D. 969.

- **Think outside the box.** Try to find playtime in unlikely places. For example, standing in line together at the grocery store or the bank, in the car going anywhere, walking the dog together, cooking, or cleaning (yes, even housework can be made into a game). You still need to schedule regular time together as a family, but don't miss the opportunities that life presents, either.

- **Schedule a play date.** We schedule just about every activity in our lives. Why not pull out the Palm Pilot and pencil in playtime? Leave work a little early once a month to get home in time to join your kids in a game of softball or to draw chalk murals on the sidewalk in front of your house (my personal favorite!). You don't even need to tell your family your plan—let it be a surprise. But if you do tell them, make sure you keep your date! Any time you tell your child you are going to do something, including play, you need to keep your word.

- **Make play a family priority.** Once you understand how important playing together can be for building your family relationships (see the following "The Benefits of Play to Family Life" section), you will want to make sure everyone in your family comes together on a regular basis to enjoy each other's company. Although a weekly Family Activity Night would be ideal, it's not always realistic, especially as your children get older. Sunday afternoon or evening is a good time to reserve for family. Hopefully, attending church together has put you "in tune" spiritually. Starting the week off with a fun activity—games or crafts—could set the tone for how you relate to each other all week long. A once-a-month half-day Saturday reserved just for family games is another option. You might need to be flexible and creative about the *when*, but make sure it happens.

How to Cultivate a Playful Attitude

Have you ever noticed how uninhibited children are in their play? A friend of mine was telling me that her three-year-old has been a superhero for about a month now. He is so intent in his play that he insists on being called only by his superhero name and will wear nothing but his superhero outfit. In fact, she can get his superhero boots off of him only after he is sound asleep. Isn't that delightful?

As grown-ups we've lost our playful edge. We need to find again the child within and cultivate an attitude that allows us to play when our children invite us to join in. James Oppenheim said, "The foolish man seeks happiness in the distance, the wise grows it under his feet." What we need is a fresh way of looking at old attitudes.

Here are some says to change your attitude:

- **Stop worrying about what other people think.** When we are so concerned about what other grown-ups might think that we pass up an opportunity to bring delight to the hearts of our children by joining in their play, something is sadly awry with our thinking. Chances are what those other grown-ups are really thinking is "I wish I were brave enough to do that with my kids!"

Family Ties

In our busyness, it is tempting as parents to give our children toys instead of our time. But only time spent together can build a strong, happy family. Children need our *presence* more than our *presents*.

If you can give your son or daughter only one gift, let it be enthusiasm.

—Bruce Barton

- **Learn to enjoy losing.** Ouch! In our competitive culture, that's a tough one. But if we make winning or losing the game secondary to the relationship we are building with our families, then we can learn to lose the game because we know we are winning something of far greater value.

- **Set the sillies free.** Many of us grew up in a time when parents thought that if they acted silly in front of their children, their children would not respect them. We need to let go of that notion. Being silly with your kids makes you more accessible to them—Mom and Dad are real people and they're fun! Respect is built on consistency, integrity, and trust. Having fun together can't hurt!

- **Don't keep thinking there will be a better time.** We constantly hear this message from the pulpit regarding our devotional life. It applies to family life as well. We have our children at home with us for such a short time. If your children are young, it may be hard to imagine that there will come a day when they don't even want to be in the same room with you. But it will come! Take the time now to make happy memories that will bind you together through even the toughest of times.

The Benefits of Play to Family Life

You've probably heard the saying "The family that prays together stays together." What about the family that plays together? Besides being nice rhyming words, pray and play have something else in common—both are activities that connect people. Here are some of the benefits to being a playing family:

That's the Spirit

"A cheerful heart is good medicine, but a broken spirit saps a person's strength." (Proverbs 17:22)

Science is just now discovering what God has known all along—joy and laughter are an important part of living a healthy life. Our joy is not only supposed to be in the Lord but in our family as well.

def·i·ni·tion Plain and Simple

First discovered in 1975, **endorphin** is one of several morphinelike substances (opioids) discovered within our brains and are manufactured by the body to reduce stress and relieve pain. Some foods, including chocolate and chili peppers, are endorphin-producing, along with exercise, relaxation, and laughter.

- The family that plays together is spending time together. There's no "a-ha" here. It's important to remember that for family relationships to grow and be strong, you need to spend time interacting with one another.

- The family that plays together knows each other better. While playing together, individual personalities—strengths and weaknesses—are revealed. Play encourages even Mom and Dad to step out of their normal roles and be themselves.

- The family that plays together remains teachable. Play is a form of learning, no matter how old you are. By playing together, everyone in the family must maintain a teachable attitude—and being teachable is important to success in life.

- The family that plays together practices communication. Every game you play requires some form of communication. Playing together helps all the family members learn and practice communications skills that make for healthy relationships.

- The family that plays together is healthier physically, mentally, emotionally, and spiritually. By engaging your family in a wide range of games, you provide a workout for their bodies and intellects while they are flexing their emotional and spiritual muscles of cooperation, teamwork, fair play, and honesty.

Guess What?

Scientific studies have conclusively demonstrated that humor contributes to physical health in measurable ways: muscle relaxation, reduction of stress hormones, immune system enhancement, pain reduction, cardiac exercise, reduced blood pressure, and improved respiration.

A Note to Single Parents

Being a single parent is the toughest job in the world. Regardless of how you came to be a single parent, parenting in a single parent home has many challenges. Time and finances are tight, and you and your children are no doubt stressed. So thinking about family playtime might feel a little overwhelming. Let me encourage you—there are a lot of things your children will have to learn to live without, but don't let laughter shared with a loving parent be one of them.

All the benefits listed for family activity time apply to your family, too. You *can* find the time to play and it doesn't have to cost a lot of money. It will help reduce stress and build your family relationships. And it provides many teachable moments for you to pass on to your children—Christian values that are important to you.

Here are some additional ideas to help you make the most of your family playtime:

- **Keep it simple.** Delegate responsibilities to your children like preparing a snack, setting up the game, and cleaning up.

 Family Ties

As you model how to play for your children and encourage siblings to play with each other—spanning age levels—you are not only creating family harmony but you are also teaching them an important parenting skill for when they have children of their own.

- **Don't overplan.** Got a night without homework? Pull out a game. Don't feel like everything has to be planned. Make it easy on yourself.
- **Get together with others occasionally.** Invite another single parent family to join you or ask Grandma and Grandpa over. Having another adult around will be good for you and the kids.
- **Relax!** If something has to go undone for another day or two, so what? Your kids won't remember that you were a day late with the laundry, but they will remember that you felt they were worth spending time with.

Practical Suggestions for Play

Playtime in any context is invaluable time for parents to spend on the child's level, engaging in activities in which the child can successfully and intimately participate. This is the spirit of family play.

Infants

Here are some ideas for infant play:

- Old standbys, such as peek-a-boo. Babies love faces, and they love to discover the face will come back.
- Itsy Bitsy Spider, Busy Bee, Pat-a-Cake, and other action songs help the child make hand play stimulating and are good for coordination.
- Read books and learn to animate your voice as you read.
- Stacking games build eye-hand coordination through interaction with their environment.
- Simple Hide and Seek. Hide in plain view behind a chair—an extension of Peek-a-Boo.
- Practice animal sounds.

Toddlers to Two-Year-Olds

Here are some ideas for this group:

- Animal sounds and behavior. How does an elephant walk? What does a flamingo look like? What does the lion say?
- Building games and puzzles are great for special development.
- Interactive storytelling. For example, "Did the spider really try to climb up again?" As the child becomes more verbal, encourage more and more input. This interaction makes long waits at restaurants go much faster.
- Dance to the music. I once had a friend who woke her children with marching music. She used the same theme whenever they needed to step up their progress toward the door. She generally tended to be on time.
- Start art! Introduce simple crafts and remember it's the process (not the outcome) that matters.

Ideas for Preschoolers

Some ideas for preschoolers:

- Mud cakes and castles. They're not good to eat, but they're excellent life skill builders and, most of all, fun. Kids get clean eventually—put the designer clothes away and let them put their whole selves into it.
- Role playing. Start a box full of interesting and versatile costumes that are different sizes, ready for whomever might drop by … including Daddy or Mommy.
- Rhyming games and songwriting about all sorts of things—the sillier the better.
- Label the house. The process itself can even be like a scavenger hunt: table, Daddy's chair, piano, messy room.
- Weave a conversation. Using long pieces of variously colored string, teach children to take turns in a conversation. Have the string balled, and whoever is talking holds the ball. When someone else picks up the conversation, let out the string and pass it to the new speaker. All must hold on to their part of the string until the end to see how the conversation weaves and knots.
- Make up silly stories about objects in your house and people in your family, giving characters the funniest of names.
- Pantomime. It's amazing how much fun you can have playing without words.

Ideas for Kids Age Six and Up

As children get older and develop their social skills, they will naturally want to spend more time playing with their peers. Clearly this is a positive development; the older the kids become, the more independent they are—that's the way God intended it to be. But don't lose touch with the importance of parents' playtime with the kids. With their growing independence comes a potential for taking the path of least resistance by simply sending them off to play with others. Play needs to be an integral part of the family as children grow older.

- Board games. The variety of board games available today is tremendous. There are board games for every age level including games for nonreaders. There are also the classics like Checkers, Dominoes, and Parcheesi.

- Cardboard boxes. We once built an entire cardboard hotel in our basement from appliance boxes. My nine-year-old was the innkeeper, taking reservations and assigning rooms, but we all joined in the fun. I actually enjoyed about 10 minutes of quiet time in my private room.
- Outdoor games such as Kick the Can and Dodge Ball are family favorites. Use a soft rubber or foam ball for safety.
- Ping-Pong is a good game for pre-teens and teens.
- Read, read, read. Besides reading storybooks together, use the shared stories to put on puppet plays or small theatrical productions that can include the whole family. You might even want to capture it on video.
- Strategy games and puzzles.

Play with a Purpose

Games and play can and should be used to teach. But here are some things that you should keep in mind:

- **Be flexible.** You might have a plan, but don't miss opportunities that come up in the process.
- **Be conscientious and thoughtful.** Never make a child feel stupid or a failure in your attempt to teach him something.
- **Keep it simple.** Don't force complicated truths into your playtime. That is not the point. Most of the time you will be sowing seeds of truth that can be cultivated later.
- **Don't preach.** Let your children learn from what they observe in your behavior.

What kinds of values can you teach while playing as a family? Take a look at what your child may be thinking during play and the value it translates into:

- **Self-worth.** I'm important enough for Mom and Dad to spend time with me.
- **Respect for others.** If I compromise it will be more fun for everyone.
- **Truthfulness.** It's not right to cheat. God is watching, too.
- **Responsibility.** I need to learn and follow the rules in order to play.

- **Patience.** I can wait for my turn.
- **Self-control.** If I lose, I will be a good sport and if I win, I will not brag.
- **Love of family.** Hey! My family is fun to be with!

Lessons of love given unconditionally are what children need most. As always when relating to your children, let your thoughts and actions be guided by the Holy Spirit through prayer. Keep your words and actions balanced by the fun and wonder of just being together.

Chapter 2

The Importance of Rules

Rules, rules, rules! Whether it is in sports, school, or play, teaching your children how to play by the rules is an important life lesson. Games are more enjoyable if everyone who is playing knows and understands the rules of play and practices them. What is so fascinating about many of the games we play today is that there are often no instruction books—sometimes they're not included and sometimes they get misplaced—yet somehow we know how to play them anyway. We learn from family, friends, teachers, and coaches.

In this chapter, we will take a look at why rules are important and how they can make playing games more enjoyable. It doesn't matter if you follow the rules that the game came with or if you make up your own rules; what really matters is that everyone agrees on what the rules are and follows them. We'll take a look at how to avoid trouble and keep the peace, how to be a good winner and a good loser, and how you can settle arguments that arise in the course of playing your game. By being clear on the rules of the game, you're sure to maximize your fun at all times!

Setting the Rules

When I was a kid, we played a schoolyard game called Champ—otherwise known as Four Square. It was played in a large square, which was painted on the ground in our schoolyard. This square was divided into four smaller squares, with one square dedicated to the "Champ." One person was the Champ and stood in the Champ's square. The object was to keep a rubber ball bouncing into each square using the palm of your hand. If you hit the ball outside the line, you were out and someone else took your place. The object was to knock the Champ out of the game, so you could move into his square.

The most interesting thing that I remember about this game is that there was always at least one kid who knew the rules—and we made up many new rules as we went along. Sometimes the new rules stuck and were passed on to the next group of kids. The rules were always announced at the beginning of recess and the game went on through recess. Sometimes we'd pick up where we left off the day before— we'd even mark our places in the waiting line. There was always a line; after all, only four people could play at a time.

The point of the story is that when you decide to play any game, it's important to establish the rules in advance. Most board games come with their own instruction books, so that's easy enough. Read the rules aloud and discuss them as you go along so everyone knows what to expect when the game begins. There are many games that are passed down to us that have no written instructions. This book will help clear up the confusion on these games, so read on. When you're ready to play the game with your family, read the rules out loud for everyone.

Plain and Simple

A set of **rules** is a prescribed guide for conduct, telling you how to proceed with your next course of action.

Setting the rules and getting everyone to agree on them is the first step to avoiding arguments when the competition begins. When playing with younger children, explain the rules in simple terms instead of reading them to ensure everyone understands. Making sure that everyone is clear on the rules is the way to fun and fair play. If you're a frequent player of games without written rules, keep a log handy on how you play and add to this log as you redefine the games with new rules.

Sometimes it's even fun to make up your own rules—changing how you start, how you win, how you keep score. Why not make your own book of family rules? Keep a notebook in your game closet that lists all of the specifics of the rules your family has agreed upon for the games you play. Besides listing the name of the game and the new rules, date each entry and have all game participants add their names. Your family rule book now serves two purposes: It is a written record of the rules you have all agreed to play by, and it is a testament to time spent together as a family.

Family Ties

If your family has a unique way of playing a familiar game, try renaming the game. Then whenever you play your unique family version, you will be making a special family memory.

Keeping the Peace

Now that you've set the rules, you're ready to play the game! Whether you're a kid or an adult, you know that when you play a game and the rules are not clear with all the players, arguments abound. But there are other factors that can suck the fun out of family fun time. Let's look at a few attitudes and actions that can turn game night into a nightmare.

Competition: The Name of the Game

When you're in competition, you see all sorts of sides to people you might otherwise not have known were there. Maybe someone in your family just *has* to win at everything. The perpetual winner can often radiate a smugness that is nothing short of nauseating. But let little brother or sister start to win and a fierceness can erupt that transforms a normally cooperative child into a monster. Accusations of "NOT FAIR!" are hurtled like poisonous barbs. That can ruin a perfectly good game and possibly the rest of the day.

Plain and Simple

A **referee** is someone who is chosen as the official, having final authority in administering a game. The ref makes the call when an action is questioned.

Because the whole idea of playing games together is to build family unity, it might be a good idea to include a code of conduct in your family rule book. You're thinking *You mean have rules for game behavior?* Absolutely. When conflicts arise—and they will—having a written code will help to mediate disputes quickly and stop harmful words and actions before they can hurt. Start with the code listed here, adapting it to reflect the ages of the children in your family and any particular family values you wish to emphasize during game play. Be sure to take time to explain the meaning of each point so that all family members understand what is expected of them.

Code of Conduct for Game Play

Everyone wants to win, but not everyone can win every game. We can all be winners if our goal is to have fun and play fair.

If something happens during the game that makes me angry, I will count to 10 and then use words to let the others know how I feel.

I will do my best to be happy when someone else is winning because that is how I want others to act when it is my turn to win.

I will finish any game I have agreed to play unless everyone decides to switch games or stop playing.

I will abide by the decisions of the referee without arguing.

I will be a gracious winner—not bragging or proud, but encouraging to other players.

I will play with honor—without cheating or showing bad attitudes.

This book will outline some major game rules, so you'll have the necessary guidance for most games, but there will be games not listed. And some rules are open to interpretation. With kids, it's almost inevitable that a fight or two will break out in the middle of the game. But kids are easy. They argue, pout for a while, and then usually move on to the next event.

But then there are the adults. Adults almost always strive to win. As parents, remember that you are playing with children and your behavior and ambitions need to be in check. By modeling the balance between competition, integrity, and graciousness, you are teaching your children an essential life lesson. Remember: The whole point is to have a good time and build family ties!

Try this: Agree before each game begins to abide by the rules and code of conduct. Choose a referee to mediate any disagreements. This doesn't always have to be the parent. Children who understand the responsibility and can reason fairly should also be given the opportunity to perform this role.

Dare to Play Fair

When children play games, squabbles arise over the rules all the time. Depending on the age group, many kids are not likely to read the rules before starting the game. They try to depend on their memory of how the game is played, and they often fall into the temptation to adjust their memory of the rules to their own benefit.

Defining "fair" is difficult even for adults at times, so you can imagine how children sometimes lose sight of it in favor of winning. The point of playing fair is not just to avoid arguments and disputes but to teach the importance of values—like honesty—in all we do.

Get Involved

Get the kids into good game-playing habits. Start by helping them set up the game, whether it's a board game or a lawn game. Check to see that everyone understands the rules. You play the role of referee initially and tell the kids that all disputes will be settled by you. You may want to set a limit on the number of disputes per game. If you hear more than this number, the game will be stopped and the kids will have to find something else to do. This is a great way to get kids to work out their own conflicts and practice self-control. If they know they can only bring three to the referee, the rest of the disputes will have to be worked out among themselves, and they'll have to choose if getting their way is more important than finishing the game.

Teach Not to Cheat

But even more likely than squabbles over the rules of a game are squabbles over cheating. I love playing board games with kids because I'm intrigued by the many ways they "strategize."

In our culture, cheating seems to be a way of life. From stories of corporate corruption to insider training to fixed sporting events—you and your children cannot avoid cheaters. But that doesn't mean you should join their ranks! It may seem to some people that cheating in a simple child's game is not significant—but wrong is wrong. By allowing children to cheat sometimes, you expose them unnecessarily to making poor decisions about cheating in the future. Make it a hard and fast rule—no cheating! If someone is caught cheating, he will have to forfeit the game, or at the very least, forfeit a turn.

While cheating is a definite "no-no," there are many games that involve bluffing—misleading your opponent in order to give yourself an advantage in the game. You may need to explain the difference to younger children. Even the most basic of children's card games may involve bluffing as part of the strategy. One of these classic card games is called I Doubt It!

To play I Doubt It, you need a minimum of three players. The more players involved, the harder the game. You deal out an entire deck of cards to all the players, and each person takes a turn placing a card face-down in the center of the table—calling out the number and suit of the card as he does so. Each player must put down a card in ascending order, but not necessarily in the same suit. You must call the card aloud as you place it face-down.

Inevitably, you will come to one person who does not have the required card to put down. So that person must bluff about what card he or she is putting down. It's up to the other players to catch the bluffer. If you suspect a bluff, you must call out "I doubt it!" on that player's turn. When the card is displayed, if the player who called "I doubt it!" is correct, the bluffer must pick up all the cards on the table. If the player who calls "I doubt it!" is incorrect, then he or she must pick up all the cards. The object of the game, of course, is to get rid of all your cards.

Even after you have made a point of teaching against cheating, be sure that someone will test the rule at some point. There is no need to humiliate the player who is caught cheating—that is no more God-honoring than the cheating. Simply enforce the no-cheating rule and move on. If the offense occurs during a family game night, do not exclude the cheater from being with the family even if he or she cannot finish the game. Let him keep score and include him in the next game or round of play.

 That's the Spirit

Humor is a rubber sword—it allows you to make a point without drawing blood.
—Mary Hirsch

If conflicts do arise during your family game time, try to defuse the situation with a little humor. You must address inappropriate behavior but you don't want anyone to walk away from your family time feeling worse than he did before.

Be a Winner!

There's nothing worse than a sore loser. Sore losers are considered whiners and bad sports. The worst kind of sore loser is one who goes around accusing everyone of cheating because he or she can't face the fact that they might not have played the game well—or that maybe luck was not on their side this time. It's best to accept the loss and try to figure out a better strategy for the next game, or better yet, accept their loss and applaud the winner.

This is an important lesson to teach your children, and it's not an easy one. In teaching a child to applaud the winner and accept his or her loss, you are teaching them a form of empathy. It feels good to win, and isn't it nice to be congratulated for your efforts? Remind your child that the next time he or she wins, he or she will receive the same praise and that they should treat others the way they would expect to be treated in return. Life is full of tough, competitive situations, and if you teach your children to stand tough when the odds are against them, you will be giving them a great gift that will help them throughout their lives—from childhood to adulthood.

While nobody likes a sore loser, the worst kind of game player is a bad winner. The person who wins the game should sit back and smile on the inside. To applaud yourself in front of everyone else and sing your own praises is bad sportsmanship. It's best to be humble about it—you know you won and everyone else knows you won, and therein lies the glory. I've played many a game with a bad winner. They are the ones who can only feel good about their accomplishment if they make everyone else feel lousy about their shortcomings. Those are the kind of people you might not want to play with again. It makes the game much more fun and certainly creates an atmosphere of fair and fun gaming if winners are humble and losers don't let their egos get in the way of an otherwise good game.

Settling Disputes

Whenever people gather in the spirit of competition, some disagreements are bound to spring up. And don't assume that it will always be the children who do the arguing. Here are some tips for settling conflicts that arise when playing games.

Talk Among Yourselves

Discuss with your family how each of your actions affects the others, both positively and negatively. Show with real-life examples how sore losers and bad winners or cheating and name calling make each player feel while playing games. Is it fun or does it put a damper on the day?

Guess What?

Edmond Hoyle (1672–1769) was the Englishman who wrote about the rules, strategies, and standard practices of card play, backgammon, chess, and other games of his time. His writings are still foundational in many of the current books of rules for games. It was probably Whist players consulting his rules who first coined the phrase "according to Hoyle." Today that phrase means to conform to standard practice or accepted procedures.

Discuss with your family the importance of rules and the need for having a fair way to settle disputes. When disputes arise, take the opportunity to sit down and work out a fair compromise. Stop the game and focus on the situation at hand. It's a wonderful opportunity to teach your children life skills. Discuss decisions you make and help the children learn to find that middle ground.

Try role-playing with your family to see if you can come up with creative ways to settle disputes. Role-play situations presented by your children—situations they might have actually encountered while playing with friends. Discuss solutions with them and summarize the need to stick to what is right and fair even when it might not be the popular choice.

Chapter 3

From Start to Finish

Kids nowadays don't play outside as much as they did in the past unless they are participating in an organized sport. Even as play has moved indoors for today's children, games now are electronic—video games, computer games, and handheld electronic games. But computer-companionship is certainly no match for human contact. And the content of electronic games needs to be carefully monitored. Virtual reality is about fantasy; reality is about using all our senses and enjoying the physical presence of other human beings. You can't avoid technology or the media, but you can limit its impact on the time you spend together as a family.

Creating the Tie That Binds

Parents who initiate a family game night when the children are young are building important communication links for those years when the kids would rather die than play games with their parents. So turn off the television, video, and computer, and start playing together. There is very little involved in setting up for most games. And although cleanup can take a little more time, you'll find out in this chapter that both setup and cleanup can also play a part in the fun.

Sizing Up the Competition

If you are like most parents today, one of the greatest challenges to your family time is the media—TV, music, video games, Internet, and so on. Two recent studies by the Annenbergy Public Policy Center of homes with children ("Media in the Home" and "Is the Three-Hour Rule Living Up to Its Potential?") and a third study ("Public Policy, Family Rules and Children's Media Use in the Home") yielded the following facts on family media use:

- Most families with children between the ages of 2 and 17 have a television, a VCR (97 percent), a computer (70 percent), and a video game player (68 percent) in the home; 52 percent have Internet access.

- Although parents are concerned about their children's television usage, here's what you will find in the bedrooms of children between 8 and 16 years old: 57 percent have a television set; 39 percent have video game equipment; 36 percent have cable service; 32 percent have a telephone; 30 percent have a VCR; 20 percent have a computer; and 11 percent have access to the Internet.

- The number of families with Internet access has more than tripled, going from 15 percent in 1996 to 52 percent in 2000. Across all media, use among children is growing.

- The more time children spend watching TV, the more time they spend using other media.

- Despite the fact that children are likely to spend four and a half hours per day in front of some form of video screen—television, computer, or video game—parents are more concerned about media content than they are about the time children spend using media.

A Basis for Bonding

Spending time with your children will allow you to find out things about your kids that you might not have known before. If your family dynamic is currently that everyone goes to his own space in your home to listen to music, watch TV, or play on the computer, you might have a bit of a struggle at first getting everyone unplugged—but give it a try. If you succeed, you'll be pleasantly surprised.

> **Family Ties**
>
> Don't buy into the myth that it is not the quantity of time you spend with your kids, it's the quality. It's clearly *both!* Playing together as a family forges ties of communication and cooperation. Sure, it's easier to let Mom, Dad, and the kids go their own way sometimes. But if you truly want to build a strong family, you need to make it a point to spend time together when you can focus on each other.

Get 'Em Young

The trick to avoiding difficulty with teenagers is to start playing games with them when they are little kids. Keep the lines of communication with them open. Talk and listen when they are little, and never stop. Always make yourself available to them. There's no better way to establish a rapport than to get down and dirty with them in a good old-fashioned game: Chess, Checkers, board games, card games, Ping-Pong, or Darts—anything that will keep the interaction alive.

This is not only important for family interaction later on, but also for their interpersonal development. Don't let them drift away into virtual reality. Keep them stimulated. Find common ground. Find out what they like and try to be involved. If they don't want you to be involved, just make sure they know you are always there to listen, help, and guide them in God's way.

Parents are busy—most parents work. It's hard to get a second to yourself and so easy to let the computer, the TV, and the music world baby-sit your kids so you can get a good hour or two of peace after a hard day. But the quality of life you build with your family is critical to their development and, ultimately, everyone's happiness. Talk to your kids, listen to your kids, but mostly play, play, play with your kids!

Keen Kids

There's no better way to engage your teenagers than with a pool table, Ping-Pong table, or dartboard. It's worth spending the money on these games. Most teens will love a competitive, action-filled game. They spend so much time sitting in class and studying for exams, not to mention just trying to figure out what they want and who they are, that a game involving skill and energy will be a nice break from their daily, intensive lifestyle. You might find it hard to pull them away and get them back to the books!

Little kids will always want to play a game—so get them while they're young! Any game you teach them will be fine with them. Whether it's a board game, card game, or word game. Kids just want to be included. If you can get them to learn a thing or two in the process, go for it! If you can have fun and educate at the same time, you can't go wrong.

Chess is a good example of a great teaching tool to use on your kids. They will be forced to learn about patience, structure, and strategy. It's a great way to sit and spend some time with children, too. While you're both leaning into the board, planning your next moves, you can also … talk. Chess is a wonderful game for kids of all ages, because not only does it force them to think ahead, memorize moves, and be still for minutes at a time, but it also forces them to think about cause and effect. "If I do this, such and such might happen." That's a very valuable tool. Think about all the biblical principles connected to our understanding of that!

> **That's the Spirit**
>
> Family game nights are wonderful opportunities to share with your family—not only to *talk* about events, but to participate together in activities that help you pass on principles that build godly character and the family values that unite you. "The wise person makes learning a joy …." (Proverbs 15:13)

Mixed Bag

If you have a family with kids of different age groups, you can try a number of different ways to get everyone involved. There are plenty of board games and card games that are good for people of all ages. I played Hearts, Spades, and Poker as a kid. I loved a good round of Double Solitaire, and Blackjack was always a favorite of mine. My strategy might not have been the greatest at the age of nine, but I certainly enjoyed playing. My siblings and I had stacks of board games, and my sister and I even invented our own. We built the game board out of a piece of cardboard, borrowed the dice and playing pieces from another game, and used index cards for draw cards. I can't remember what the game was, but because we played so many different board games, we were savvy enough to create our own.

> **Family Ties**
>
> Invent your own game as a family! Break out art supplies and put on your thinking caps. Try to come up with a new board game or create a new game of cards. The act of creating the game may be more fun than actually playing the game, but one thing is sure—you will be creating a precious family memory.

My sister's favorite board game was Masterpiece—a game where you actually bid, auction-style, on postcards of famous paintings. This game was my first introduction to art. I learned names like Whistler, Degas, Monet, Van Gogh, and Picasso. The whole family used to play, and my parents, both educators, told us about the paintings we were bidding on. It was educational and always fun. With a game like that, even if you don't know a lot about art, you can look up the paintings in the library with your children later. When I was older, my parents took us to museums and I recognized some of the artwork because of that game. That's pretty amazing!

Guess What?

The auction game Master-piece was released in 1970 by Parker Brothers. In 1996, Hasbro re-released it, but it seemed to have lost a lot of its popularity. Another art auction game was High Bid, which was set in an art antiques auction. High Bid was released by 3M.

That's the Spirit

Be humble and gentle. Be patient with each other, making allowances for each other's faults because of your love.

—Ephesians 4:2

I love this verse for families, especially if you replace the word *faults* with *differences*. Family members have a lot in common but they are still a bunch of unique individuals living, loving, and laughing together under the same roof.

In order not to exclude anyone from family game night, try organizing the family into teams. If there's a child who might be too young to play a certain game, make sure that child is teamed up with an older player. Most children will be happy just to be involved—but there will come a time when the child will notice that he or she is the only one paired up and will ask to play on his or her own. If the child is still too young, just let him or her be on his or her own and adapt the rules so they feel involved. It's not about playing a perfect game; it's about having a good time and making everyone feel good.

Take It Outside

Family game time shouldn't be restricted to indoors. Far too few Americans—both adults and children—get outdoors as often as we should. Regardless of the season, there is some game you can play outdoors. In the fall there is touch football, kick ball, or your own family version of soccer. Snow is no excuse! Try a game of tag or Frisbee golf out in the white stuff. In the spring, there's softball, and summer weather is perfect for a whole host of outdoor games. There's definitely truth to the adage "families that play together, stay together." It's important for families to let off steam, express their love for each other, and just have a good time through whatever games they enjoy playing.

Choosing Sides: Team Games

It's important to be as fair as possible when choosing sides in games. If your family is engaging in a game of skill, try to be balanced about the ages of the people on the teams. If it's a game of luck, try mixing up the age groups; it won't really matter.

In the home, you might want to pair a child with an adult or a teen with a child. You obviously don't want two adults against two children—that wouldn't be fair. Sometimes the kids want to play against the adults, and if they insist, then go for it. It might be fun. Sometimes you'll be surprised how much the kids know and more surprised when they beat the pants off you!

For group games, I think it's best to pull names from a hat. Write everyone's name down on a piece of paper; fold the papers and mix them in a hat or bag of some kind. Names should be pulled out one at a time and teams divided accordingly.

There are many different ways to create teams. At some birthday parties I've attended, a parent would simply divide the room in half. Wherever you were standing determined what team you were on. You can give out name tags or stickers as guests arrive that designate a team by color or symbol. For example, animal stickers are great for children's groups. You can have four or five stickers of a lion for one team, four or five stickers of giraffes, etc. Calling all lions together into a team is then a fun and easy task. In outdoor games where there was usually no adult supervision, we used one of the rhyming methods (see Chapter 5 for more on birthday party games) to pick who is "It." You can quickly have everyone number off according to how many teams are needed for the activity.

What Shall We Play?

This might be the trickiest part of family game night—unless you've been playing for a while and have established the family favorites. Some family members are bound to develop some favorites they want to play over and over (especially if they often win at that game!). There are a couple ways to be fair in your decision-making.

Consider all the game options. Try to come up with a list of games that everyone is willing to play, even though they may not be totally excited about every one.

Another method is to put all the games in a hat—including the ones that some family members are not so excited about having as an option. Have someone pull the name of the game out of the hat, and that is the game that you wind up playing that night—no matter who likes it and who doesn't. Make sure the kids are aware of this rule in advance and that cheerful cooperation is expected.

You can also put a schedule up on the wall and designate each game night to one of the children. For example, Monday is Tara's night and Friday is Matthew's night. What about Joey? Well, he will get the following Monday night. Create the schedule months in advance so that the kids are clear on which night is their night.

When it's their night, they are responsible for picking the game, setting up the game, and cleaning up the game. By using this method, you are teaching the kids leadership skills. They are setting the tone for the night in the game that they choose, and in being the leader, they have certain responsibilities like setup and cleanup. Kids do much better with structure and guidance. If they know what's coming, they know what to do and you'll avoid conflict altogether.

Try to make the responsibility of game night an honor, maybe even a reward earned during the week. Add a little fun by designating a "King" or "Queen" for family night. The game night leader might be responsible for gathering all supplies and setting up the game, calling together family members, and choosing what snack will be served. If the honor rotates on a regular basis, make it a rule that whoever leads the family night one week is responsible for cleanup the following week. Rotating responsibilities promotes a servantlike attitude between family members.

Game's Over

Starting and ending family game time well is important to the overall experience you are trying to create. Whether you decide to make setup and cleanup a group activity or have individual family members be responsible for those tasks, either mom or dad will need to organize it and provide some guidance. Sharing the responsibility for family games is just one more way to help your children develop life skills.

There is no game without some element of mess. Some games require more tools than others, so there is more cleanup involved. Never, ever clean up the game without the kids' involvement. This is not just about fun for them—it's a complete package.

It's a good idea to have the whole family clean up the game together. If it's a board game, one child can be responsible for sorting the play money and stacking it up neatly back in the box. If it's a little kid, he can use the opportunity to practice his numbers and colors. Another child can sort the draw cards and put them neatly back in the box, while yet another child or adult can put the dice and playing pieces away. It should be a group effort.

If you decide to designate a family game night to each child, you could make that child responsible for choosing the game, as well as setting up and cleaning up. Even though that child is responsible for everything, don't leave the child on his or her own to take care of it all. That could make responsibility feel very unrewarding. Responsibility shouldn't feel like a drag or a chore—it should be somewhat empowering. So what you can do is have that child be responsible for the setup and cleanup, but make that responsibility about delegating and recruiting help for the task.

The trick to setup and cleanup is preparing your children in advance. Tell them beforehand that playing the game means you also have jobs. If they expect this, you'll have less griping when it comes time to do the work. The responsible child must delegate cleanup chores to the other family members. He or she should assign tasks to all the other players, but is ultimately responsible for the whole game being put away successfully. They may need a little guidance.

Setup is usually not a problem because the kids are so excited to play. Cleanup is the drag—they've already had their fun and now they want to walk away. Just let them know in advance that everyone has a responsibility, and if they are not willing to clean up, then no one is going to play.

Shhhh! Quiet Time

Ahh … the game is put away, the children are hooted-and-hollered-out, and you can finally put your feet up and relax. Well … not quite! The game is put away, the kids are wired and dying for another game, and you're pulling your hair out. Again—it's all about preparing your kids in advance.

Before you play any game, make sure the kids are fed, homework is done, they are bathed and in their pajamas ready for bed. When the game is put away, maybe it's early enough for a half-hour of TV, or maybe you want to pull out a book and read to them for a little while. One way or another, you have to set a few rules for family game night.

You can start with these guidelines, and depending on how it all develops with your particular family, you may want to make up your own rules as you go along. Just get started with a plan and see how it goes. Here's a list that might help:

- If family game night is on a weeknight, homework must be done, and everyone must be clean and in their jammies ready for bed.
- Everyone helps set up.
- Everyone helps clean up.
- There is one game allowed per night.
- The game must end by a certain time.
- If there's still time before bed, it is called "quiet time," when everyone mellows out until it's time for bed.
- If kids do not adhere to quiet time, there will be no family game night next week.

It's all about establishing a routine, setting rules, being clear, and sticking to all the rituals. If you do, you'll find that the kids will get used to it and settle in pretty easily.

When the kids are finally tucked away after a good night of playing, you can finally kick back and relax—or you can pull out the cards and have an adult game night. The kids will never have to know!

Chapter 4

Road Trip: Car Games

Kids love games, and it's amazing how the games we played as kids are now being played by our own kids. The games just keep getting passed down from generation to generation by virtue of experience. The games our parents taught us on long car rides are now being taught to the next generation of kids … and the cycle continues.

This chapter is all about car games—filling those hours in the car while you travel with the kids, on vacation, to Grandma's, wherever you need to go. Stave off the inevitable "Are we there yet?" with one of these memorable travel games for kids.

Road Trip Survival Kit

For some car games you will need to have some tools on hand to make game-playing easier. Keep packed a little kit that can slip under a seat in your car or in a pocket that attaches to the back seat. You can purchase storage pockets that strap onto the back of the front seat so that supplies are in easy reach of children in the back. Or you can buy an inexpensive apron with pockets that can be tied around the headrest and attached to the seat with Velcro dots or safety pins.

Here are just some of the things you'll want to stock in your road trip kit:

For kids three to six years old:

- Crayons
- Coloring books
- Vinyl window clings
- Picture books

For kids seven and up:

- Pen
- Pencil
- Pencil sharpener
- Paper
- Map

You should always be careful when allowing a child to use a pen or a pencil in the car. These tools should only be used by children of a certain age and always under supervision. Remember, you're in a moving vehicle and any pointed object can be dangerous.

Let's Go!

It would not be possible to take long trips with children without the use of games such as the ones discussed here. Nowadays, kids have electronic handheld games, and cars come equipped with TVs and VCRs, but every so often the kids will even get bored with these things and start to get fidgety and whiney.

Little kids will do anything to get their parents' attention and, frankly, all the TVs and videos in the world will not keep them happy for the next few hundred miles. It would be nice if the kids could just get into a good book and not want to put it down; this might happen if your kids are old enough to read—but it's that word *might* that could cause you big problems down the road if you don't have a plan B.

Family Ties

Encourage participation and cooperation among family members while traveling together. Kids and parents alike can join in the fun with many of these games, and anything that creates family interaction is a good thing.

When the books are put away, the attention spans wane, the batteries wear out, and the videos become repetitive, it's time to pull out the good old standbys. Anyone born before 1985 knows these games very well because we *had* to play them in the car. The only other electronic gadgets we had to distract ourselves with were portable cassette players or radios—if we were lucky enough to have owned them.

When you decide to take family car rides, you're taking your kids away from their friends, their bedrooms, and their regular playgrounds. It means that they are out of their element—and we all know that most kids require constant stimulation or boredom sets in very quickly. So if you're planning a long trip, you should also plan to bring along many forms of entertainment—the best of which are the games that don't require batteries. They are the games that were made up out of moments of desperation by parents and teachers—games that keep the peace for as long as everyone can keep playing. You'll want to know a few of these games because even *they* will lose their interest from hour to hour.

The history of these "car games" is virtually unknown. They have been played in various ways, in various countries, in multitudes of languages for ages. There was a time, before kids had so much electronic stimuli, that parents had to be more interactive with the kids just to manage their own levels of chaos. Now, rather than let the kids zone out, this is a great opportunity to work with them—let them use their minds, their imaginations, and their creativity, rather than just passively absorb all that information through technology.

Little kids will be thrilled to get your undivided attention, but you might have a bigger struggle with the teenagers. Rather than resort to plug-pulling to get them to zone in, maybe they'll see the younger kids having so much fun that they'll tune in for a few minutes to see what all the laughing is about. Their level of interest will depend on the level of the game, however. Maybe the games for little kids will spark some of their own memories and they'll want to teach their younger siblings a thing or two.

All supplies should be stored in a pocket, container, or compartment for safety purposes. Don't leave stuff out so it can fly around the car and hurt someone. Keep everything that is not currently in use stored away—it will help keep items from getting lost and make cleanup quicker, too.

The I Spy Games

I Spy is one of the first car games your kids will probably ever learn. It's the kind of game you start playing with kids long before the first car trip. You may have played it for the first time with your little one in the doctor's office—when you were waiting ... and waiting ... for your name to be called. It might be one of the first games that pops into your head to keep your child from getting bored. It's a great game to play one-on-one or in a group.

I Spy with One Child

If you're playing with one child, you start by saying "I spy with my little eye, something that is ..." and fill in with a color. The child is then required to guess what it is you're looking at. You can pick any color, of course. It's a great way to help your child build an understanding of colors.

When the child guesses the object, it is then the child's turn to "spy" something. You keep going back and forth, alternating turns.

If the child is a little bit older, you can use letters. "I spy with my little eye, something starting with the letter B." If the child knows some basic reading skills, you can easily play this game with him or her.

Because the view from a moving vehicle changes often, it is better to set a limit on guesses when playing I Spy in the car. Chances are that after three guesses, the object that was spied originally is already miles behind you and the chances of a player guessing correctly are greatly diminished.

You can play I Spy with more than one child very easily. One person goes first and the first person to guess the object gets to spy the next object.

Family Ties

Managing noise levels while playing some car games is a challenge. It helps to turn off any other noisemakers—radio, TV, stereo, etc.—but if the decibel level continues to climb, you can start keeping score, giving two points for correct answers but deducting a point if the answer is shouted out or if the noise level is unreasonable. Keep interest in the points high by promising to exchange cash (nickels and dimes) for points so that small purchases can be made at the next stop.

License Plate Bingo

This game works best in traffic jams because you can get a good, long look at the license plates. For License Plate Bingo, you'll need a pen and paper. Give each child a piece of paper and a pen. The kids should write the letters of the alphabet on the piece of paper. They then need to look out the window and see what letters of the alphabet they can spot on the license plates of other cars. The kids cross off each letter on their piece of paper as they see that letter on a license plate. The object of the game is to cross off all the letters and shout "Bingo!" by the time the traffic starts moving again.

To liven things up a little, you might want to give the kids different windows, on different sides of the car, to ensure that they are looking at different license plates.

To liven things up even more, tell the kids that they have to find the letters in alphabetical order. In other words, they can't just cross off the letters in any old order. You might want to resort to this if the cars haven't moved and you need a round two!

You can also try playing License Plate Bingo without paper and pencil. Just have the kids shout out the letters in alphabetical order as they see them. You can do the same thing with signs along the highway. Try reverse alphabetical order for a change of pace. Have the kids start with the letter Z and go backward to A.

Got older kids? Here's a variation of License Plate Bingo that my 21-year-old nephew taught to my 12- and 14-year-old daughters on a recent visit. They had a blast and forged a family memory we all cherish. And now my girls have started playing it with their friends.

The goal is to be the first to spot a license plate from another state—a state different from the one you are in—and be the first to call out the name of the state. However, you have to remember any states that have already been spotted and called out. There is a slight penalty for calling out a state that has been previously named. Even though my nephew is over six feet tall, our kids made the penalty a light punch in the arm and everyone survived to tell about it. But a point system works just as well.

What If

All you need for What If is some imagination and maybe a map. Some of the best games you'll ever play with your kids are games that involve creativity and imagi-nation.

Guess What?

Who knew that the Studebaker company—the famous manufacturer of automobiles started by Henry and Clement Studebaker in 1852—began as a blacksmith shop building covered wagons? The road trip 150 years ago was probably not a whole lot different than the road trips we take today. Just bumpier!

In this game, you pose a "what if" scenario to your child and he or she has to describe the conditions and possibilities.

For example, ask your child, "What if the car trip we're taking was actually in a covered wagon?" The questions the child should consider answering are things like:

- How long would the trip take?
- How many times would you have to stop to feed and water the horses?
- What would you eat?
- How much water would you need to bring?

You can look at the map with the child and try to imagine what the country looked like with single lane dirt roads. What kind of obstacles would you encounter on these roads?

A map is an excellent prop for this game. Use some of your own historical knowledge to liven up the discussion. If you have time before the trip, study up on the history a little bit and offer information to the children to liven up their imaginations and knowledge that much more. You can even bring along a couple of books on the topic. If someone else is driving, you can always look at the pictures in the book with the child and talk about what life in the "olden days" was like. If you are the only one driving, brush up on the geography before the trip with the kids, circle highlights on the map, and have the kids spot them as you continue the journey.

 That's the Spirit

There are no days in life so memorable as those which vibrate to some stroke of the imagination.

—Ralph Waldo Emerson

Games that indulge the creative spark in each of us make a lasting connection. We are made in God's image and he, being the Supreme Creator, must have an incredible imagination.

You can also set up an even more imaginative scenario: What would the trip be like if you did it a thousand years from now? Would you be traveling to other planets? What kind of vehicle would you be traveling in? What kind of fuel would it take? What would you be eating and drinking? What obstacles could you encounter? Kids will love this game. There's no history lesson to teach, just a lot of creative energy to indulge.

Camping Trip

Camping Trip is a game my friends and I used to play when we couldn't sleep at night. It can be a memory or guessing game, and for some reason, stretching my memory always made me sleepy.

There are a couple ways to play the game. You can play it as strictly a memory game or you can play so that the other players have to guess the rules of play as you go along:

The first person starts off by saying:

"I'm going on a camping trip and I'm going to bring …"

At this point the person says something he or she would want to bring on the camping trip. Let's say it's a "toothbrush." The next person would then say:

"I'm going on a camping trip and I'm going to bring a toothbrush and …" This person would then have to add something else that they would bring on the trip. But this time, the object must start with the last letter of the previous object. In the case of "toothbrush," the last letter is "h," so the person would have to think of an object that starts with an "h." Let's say the person chooses "horse."

The third person would then have to say, "I'm going on a camping trip and I'm going to bring a toothbrush, a horse, and an electric guitar." The game continues until someone forgets an object on the list. That person is out and the game continues until there is only one person left.

You can simplify this version of the game by taking away the memory element. The children don't have to repeat the other objects on the list; they just have to add another item to the list that starts with the last letter of the previous item.

Alphabetical Version

You can also play Camping Trip using objects in alphabetical order. For example: "I'm going on a camping trip and I'm going to bring an asteroid." Then "I'm going on a camping trip and I'm going to bring an asteroid, and a baseball …."

The game continues the same way until there's only one person left who didn't forget an item on the list.

Who Am I?

When I was a kid, we called Who Am I? 20 Questions. One person thinks of something—person, place, or thing—and asks, "Who am I?" To figure it out, the other players have to ask questions like:

* Are you an animal?
* Are you blue?
* Do you swim in the ocean?

The person answering should only give "yes" or "no" answers to make the game a little trickier. With little kids, you might want to allow full answers so they don't get too frustrated with the game.

What's Next?

If you're on a really long car ride and you've exhausted all other games, here are some games for the desperate parent or child.

Family Ties

In our fast-paced lives today, the object of travel is usually to get where you are going as quickly as possible. But by choosing the faster way, we may be missing out on precious times with our children that we can never recapture. Slow down! Drive instead of fly. Make the trip in two days instead of one. Though road trips can sometimes challenge our sanity, the memories they create are well worth it.

Thumb Wrestling

When all else fails, don't give up. Do not pull your hair out or resort to threats—there's always the good old thumb wrestle.

Tell the kids to put out their hands. Each kid puts out his or her right hand (or you can have each child put out his or her left hand) as though to shake hands. Instead of locking hands, though, they make their fingers into a C shape and lock fingers. Each child's thumb should be resting on the top of the "handshake." You move the thumbs back and forth over each other saying "one, two, three" and let the wrestling begin.

Another way to begin the game is for the kids to chant: "One, two, three, four—we will have a thumb war; five, six, seven, eight—try to keep your thumb straight." Then the wrestling begins.

The object is to use your thumbs in an effort to trap the other person's thumb—meaning that one person should be pressing down on the other person's thumb so that that person can't lift his thumb. The "challenge" of the game is that you cannot unclasp your fingers to maneuver your thumbs, and you cannot move your whole hand—only the thumb.

Kids are very funny people. I hear they've made up a variation since my thumb-wrestling days. It's called Snake in the Grass. It's basically just a way to cheat. One person uses his index finger to trap the thumb, saying it's a snake in the grass.

The Purse Game

This is the ultimate game of desperation. A mom can play with the kids by emptying her purse and letting the kids go through her stuff. With little kids, you have to be careful that they don't get their hands on anything they shouldn't! You can have the kids categorize the objects they see. They can group together things that are round or square. Or they can group together things that are made of paper. You can even have them categorize things that are of a certain color. This game will work with kids around the ages of four through six.

I wish my mom had played that game with us. She always carried such a huge purse full of interesting stuff. Dads might not be able to play this game with the kids unless they have a mighty interesting wallet or briefcase!

Chapter 5

Birthday Party Favorites

Birthday parties take a lot of energy, and any parent who undertakes a big party for little kids deserves a lot of credit. It really is great fun to plan a kid's party, but when you do it for the first time, you'll find it requires a lot of creativity and patience.

Nowadays, there are all sorts of theme restaurants that offer party space for kids, and that's not a bad idea if you want to keep the chaos and mess out of your house. But if you've never planned a kid's party at home, give it a try. You'll be surprised how much fun it can actually be if you're prepared.

This chapter covers classic children's party games of all kinds. From what you'll need to what to say to how to play those silly childhood games, this chapter has it all. The memories will probably start to fly as you read about Red Rover, Red Light/ Green Light, Hot Potato, and Telephone. Let the games begin!

Classic Party Games

I attended many fun birthday parties as a kid. Almost every party I attended was chock-full of the best games, cake, ice cream, goodie bags, hats, and balloons. My parents put the same kind of energy into our parties as well. Some of these games might seem too old-fashioned for today's high-tech kids, but you may be pleasantly surprised. And many of these classic party games can be used as the basis for game variations at theme-related parties.

Guess What?

There are so many wonderful rhymes associated with children's games. Does anybody remember this one?

> The wonder ball goes round and round
> To pass it quickly you are bound
> If you're the one to hold it last
> The game is past
> And you are out!
> O-U-T—out!
> —Rhyme for a version of Hot Potato

The best party I remember was my sister's sixth birthday. Her entire class plus the neighbor kids were invited. The house was packed with little girls in patent-leather shoes and boys in bow ties. After a few rounds of musical chairs, my mother laid out huge pieces of newsprint and watercolor paints and we painted while listening to tunes from Broadway musicals. We painted and painted: faces, houses, clowns, cats, dogs, cars, trees … whatever we wanted. When we were done, my mother taped the paintings all around the basement walls so everyone could admire each other's work. It was magical to walk around and look at all the beautiful colors.

Family Ties

If you plan to allow the children to engage in any potential clothes-staining crafts, tell the parents in advance that casual clothes and smocks might be in order for the occasion. You wouldn't want to send a child home in a paint-smeared party dress.

Each child was given a prize for creating a masterpiece and was allowed to take his or her picture home at the end of the party. I remember wishing we could keep all the pictures on the walls, so our gray basement would always be colorful.

The worst party I ever attended was one where the parents served watermelon for dessert. It was a large group of kids seated at several tables scattered throughout the living room, and we made a horrible mess. The party ended in a watermelon seed-spitting contest, and we were all sent home early. The little birthday girl was crying when we were shuffled out, and I don't think we ever got to the present-opening. Stick to the cake and ice cream—watermelon, and other messy foods, might not be such a good idea for an indoor party. That kind of food is just fodder for trouble-making minds!

You should have prizes on hand for the winning team members or players. Prizes can be small, inexpensive toys or even candy. Kids just like to know that there's some sort of reward at the end of the game. It makes playing even more exciting. But I also believe in consolation prizes for the kids who don't win. We don't want anyone to go home empty-handed.

What You'll Need

You will need the following supplies for your child's party:

- Chairs for Musical Chairs.
- Stereo and CDs (or radio) for Musical Chairs and Hot Potato.
- Beanbag or ball for Hot Potato.
- Appropriate clothes and shoes for outdoor games.
- Space (for both inside games and outdoor games).
- Prizes for everyone!
- "Hat," pen, and paper: You'll need these things to pick players at random. Some games require someone to be "It," in which case you will have to do some selecting. (More on being "It" coming up.) The best way is to write each child's name on a piece of paper and place the names in a "hat"—a bag, box, or other container. When a child's name has been picked, remove the name from the "hat" and don't return it. This way, you won't pick the name again and other children will have a chance to be it. It's all about fairness!

If your child's party is in the summertime, you can play most of these games outside in a backyard or even at the park. For some of the games you'll need a good amount of space, while for others you should be able to get by with moving some furniture out of the way.

Choosing "It"

I used to hate it when my parents and teachers would say, "Life isn't fair." I agree in most cases ... however, my retort was always "It can be." Whenever there's a way to make things fair for kids, you should try. The fairness issue has been around a long time in the arena of children's games, especially when it comes to choosing "It." "It" is the person who does the chasing, replying, winking, questioning—whatever the game requires of "It." Sometimes being "It" is a position of power, while other times you want to be anything but "It"—that all depends on the game.

You can try first for a volunteer—if you get none or more than one, then you will need another method for choosing. There are several rhyming games that work particularly well for choosing "It." When the rhyme is done you either have your "It" or eventually get to the "It" by process of elimination.

For all the rhymes, each child puts out a fist in front of him or herself. The person who recites the line (an adult at a party, or the "kid in charge" at an unsupervised game) taps each child on the fist with his or her own fist (they include themselves in this by tapping themselves on the chin). With each word, a child is tapped.

Here are some of the rhymes:

Engine, Engine

Engine, engine, number nine,
Going down Chicago line,
If the train falls off the track,
Do you want your money back?

The child who is tapped on the word *back* says "yes" or "no."

If the answer is "yes," the tapping child continues the rhyme by tapping "y-e-s, spells yes, and you shall have your money back." If the answer is "no," the tapping child continues the rhyming and tapping by saying, "n-o spells no, you don't get your money back."

The person who is tapped on the last word *back* is "It."

One Potato

One potato, two potato, three potato, four.
Five potato, six potato, seven potato, more.

The child tapped on *more* removes his fist, and the rhyming and tapping starts again with the remaining children. The last child to be holding out a fist is "It."

Icka Bicka

Icka bicka soda cracker
Icka bicka boo;
Icka bicka soda cracker
Out goes you.

This one is pretty self-explanatory. The last child remaining is "It."

Eenie, Meenie, Meinie, Moe

Eenie, Meenie, Meinie, Moe,
Catch a tiger by the toe,
If he hollers, let him go,
Eenie, Meenie, Meinie, Moe.

The person who is tapped on "Moe" is "It."

You can use any of these rhymes to establish who is "It" in your party games; you can also pull names from a "hat," as mentioned earlier.

I am greatly opposed to letting kids pick the teams. If you were the uncoordinated athlete in your childhood and have any recollection of your days in school gym class, you'll understand why. Kids (although they don't mean any harm) pick their friends or the best players to be on a team. This does nothing for the self-esteem of the less popular or less coordinated kids, and I think the practice is wrong. Picking teams at random is the best way to go.

Everybody Outside!

Take the fun outdoors! There are many memorable outdoor games to play at a child's party. Here are just a few.

Red Rover

Red Rover is best played outside for a summertime party. It requires a lot of space and room to run.

The game begins by picking two opposing teams, which should be done by an adult or by drawing names. Then give each team a name. You can call them the "A" and "B" teams or the "Jets" and the "Sharks"—whatever you prefer. You can pick silly names, too: Try the Weebles and the Wobbles for little kids.

The two teams should form opposing lines—facing each other—with a large space between them. Each child holds the hand of the child next to him or her to form a chain.

The team that goes first (try a simple flip of a coin to make this decision) forms a huddle to decide which member of the opposing team they want to "call over." Once they have chosen, they rejoin hands and say "Red Rover, Red Rover, we call (insert name of child chosen) over." Say that child's name is Joey. Joey then high-fives his teammates and prepares for the run, while the opposing team clasps hands as hard as they can.

> **Family Ties**
>
> You can have a really good time just picking the names for your various teams. Let the kids get really creative. The sillier the name, the more they will giggle—the more fun for everyone!

It's Joey's job to try to run as fast and hard as he can to break through the opposing team's chain. If he breaks through, he gets to go back to his team. If he doesn't, then he joins the opposition and must call over, and hold back, other members of his original team.

If Joey breaks through the line and returns to his team, his team then gets to call someone over. If Joey doesn't break through, then not only does he join the opposing team, but they get to call someone over again!

> **Family Ties**
>
> There's no need to give prizes after every game if you are providing a take-home party bag at the end of the festivities. Party bags are made up ahead of time and handed out as children leave. Enlist your family's help to transform paper lunch sacks decorated with markers to use for the bags and stuff with goodies. Choose one or two low-cost items like a small toy, puzzle, or book and then add candy, stickers, and other less-expensive items to complete the bag. Be sure to make up one or two extra bags just in case an unexpected guest drops in.

You keep playing until one team has "captured" all the players from the opposing team. Because all the children wind up on the winning team in the end, in Red Rover, everybody wins!

Red Light/Green Light

Red Light/Green Light is another great game for the outdoors. You can also play it inside, in a basement for example, if you have enough room (at least 15 to 20 feet).

In this game, one person is the "stoplight." You can choose the person by drawing names or using one of the rhyming methods. The person acting as the stoplight stands at one end of the yard with his or her back to the rest of the players. There should be about 15 feet between the stoplight and the players.

With his or her back to the others, the stoplight says "green light" which gives the go-ahead for players to start walking toward the stoplight. At any time, the stoplight may say "red light" and turn around quickly to spot anyone who doesn't stop in time. If the stoplight catches anyone still moving, that person is out. The stoplight points to each player who was caught moving and calls out his or her name one at a time. For example: pointing to each player one at a time, he or she says, "Tara, I saw you" and "Matthew, I saw you, too." Those children have to sit on the sidelines and watch the rest of the game.

Play resumes when the stoplight again turns his or her back to the others and says "green light." The play keeps going like this until either everyone is out or someone touches the stoplight.

If all players are caught, the stoplight wins. If someone touches the stoplight before he or she turns around, that player is the winner.

What's the Time, Mr. Wolf?

For this game, one child is chosen to be the wolf. The wolf stands about 10 feet away with his or her back to the rest of the children. The children call out in unison: "Mr./ Ms. Wolf, what time is it?" The wolf returns the call with a response of 1 through 12 o'clock—turning around to face the other children as he or she does so.

The children will then take as many steps as the time announced. For example: Let's say the wolf says it's 10 o'clock—the children can take 10 steps forward. There is no limit on the size step the kids can take—they can take huge steps or little steps.

When everyone has taken the number of steps required, the wolf turns his or her back to the other children again and the children cry out the same question. It keeps going this way until the wolf finally says "dinner time!" The wolf turns around and chases the children. The children have to run back to the start line. If they make it to the start line, they are safe. The wolf has to try to catch at least one person to become the next wolf.

Indoor/Outdoor Games

There's one thing you can't predict: the weather. The following games are suitable for either inside or out, making planning your party a lot less stressful.

Musical Chairs

For this game you will need several chairs. If you plan to play the game, you may need to borrow chairs from your neighbors or rent some from a local party rental supply. You'll need one less chair than children. For example, if there are 10 children at the party, you will need 9 chairs.

The chairs should be set up in a circle with the seats facing into the circle. The children should also be inside the circle. The chairs should be set up far enough apart so that the children can parade in front of them.

You will need a CD player or radio to play this game. The children start to parade in front of the chairs when the music starts. When you stop the music, the children have to scramble quickly onto the seat of a chair—only one child per chair. One child will be out because there won't be enough chairs.

Each time a child goes out, you have to remove a chair to equalize the child-to-chair ratio. There should always be one less chair than children. Eventually you will have two children and just one chair. Those last two kids will have to parade around the one chair until the music is stopped. The first one to make it onto the seat of the chair is the winner.

Too many children and too few chairs? Try this indoor variation of Musical Chairs: Instead of using chairs arranged in a circle, tape a large square of cardboard or construction paper to the floor instead of a chair—one for each child, minus one. Space the squares far enough apart so that children will not jostle each other to take possession of a square. When the music stops, players must find a square to stand in or be out.

Mother May I?

This is a game that can be played indoors or outdoors. There is no running involved.

One child stands with his or her back to the others. This person is called "Mother." (If the child is a boy, you can change it to "Father.") The children ask: "Mother/Father, may I take a step?" Each child must make the request one by one.

In response to each question, the Mother may respond in one of the following ways: "no" or "yes, you may take [number and size] steps." The Mother fills the blanks with the number and size step he or she wants each child to take.

For example, the Mother can say: "Yes, you may take three giant steps," or "Yes, you may take two baby steps," or "Yes, you may take four medium steps." If the Mother senses someone is just a little too close, she can say "no."

If the child forgets to say "Mother, may I?" he or she has to go all the way back to the starting line.

The goal is for the players to try to sneak up on the Mother and touch her.

Use one of the "It" choosing methods to start the game. The person who goes first might be placed on the far left and the turns can then move to the right. It's up to you how you want to organize it, but the key is to be as fair as possible.

In some versions of Mother May I? people make up their own steps. You can try "ballet steps," for example, where the child will have to try to do some fancy turn, or "pee wee steps," where the child can only move the tiniest possible step.

Hot Potato

This game, like Musical Chairs, is one that builds anticipation as the music starts and stops. You'll see such concentration on the faces of the kids as they pass that potato from one to another. Wait for the shrieks when the music stops. This game is fun for the kids to play and sometimes even more fun for the adults to watch. Here's how to play.

All the children either stand or sit in a circle. You can use any object as the potato. Some people really use a potato while others use a beanbag. You will need a CD player, tape deck, or radio for this game.

Turn on the music and hand the hot potato to one of the children. This child must pass the hot potato either to his or her left or right. Each child must continue to pass the potato until the music stops. When you stop the music, the child left holding the potato is out and must leave the circle. The children will shriek with laughter and fear when the music stops. The anticipation on their faces during this game is worth the noise.

I was at a party where the family used a store-bought hot potato that looked like one of those cartoon cannon balls with a built-in ticker. It was quite intimidating to hear that ticker just humming away as the black plastic ball was passed quickly from child to child.

Party Games for Little Kids

Here are some games that may be appropriate for preschoolers. Not only are these games fun, but they have also proven to be educational. You'll find that kids already know some of these games from school.

For the really wee tots, try some of the following games.

 That's the Spirit

> Children are our second chance to have a great parent-child relationship.
> —Dr. Laura Schlessinger

While these games might stir fond childhood memories for many, perhaps you don't have such memories of childhood parties and games with other children. By giving your children joyful experiences, you are creating new memories not just for them, but yourself as well.

Simon Says

This game is very simple and children really love it. You'll never see them concentrate so hard!

Have the children stand facing you or another child who is deemed to be "Simon." The person playing Simon gives the other children an instruction that almost always begins with "Simon says ...."

If Simon says "Simon says touch your nose," all the children must touch their noses. Then Simon might say, "Simon says hop on one foot." All the children should then hop on one foot. Then Simon might say, "Hold up two fingers." If any of the children holds up two fingers, they are out. Why? Because Simon didn't say so. If the instruction doesn't start with "Simon says" and a child follows the instruction, he or she is out and must sit down. The last child standing gets to be the next Simon.

Duck Duck Goose

This is another game you might have learned in the classroom. My kindergarten teachers used to let us play it just before the end of the schoolday. We looked forward to it every day.

All the kids sit in a circle facing each other. One child is picked to be "It." The child who is "It" walks around the outside of the circle (the backs of the children) and touches each child on the head, saying "duck … duck … duck …." Each head touched gets a "duck." When a child is touched on the head and "It" says "Goose," the child who is the "goose" must stand up and chase "It" around the outside of the circle. "It" has to try and sit in the empty spot vacated by the goose. The goose has to try and tag "It" before "It" can sit in his or her spot. If the goose cannot tag "It," he or she becomes "It" and the duck-duck-goosing starts again.

If "It" is tagged by the goose, he or she must sit in the center of the circle. The goose then becomes "It" for the next round. The person in the center cannot move until another player is tagged—then he can take that person's spot in the circle.

Telephone or Grapevine

Telephone is a great party game for kids of all ages. I've even played it with my adult friends. It's always good for a laugh.

Everyone sits in a circle about arm's-length from each other. Someone in the circle starts by whispering a message to the person to his or her left or right. The message should only be one short sentence. The person who receives the message must then pass the message on to the person next to him or her. The last person to receive the message must deliver it aloud to the entire room. The kids will really have a good giggle when they realize just how misconstrued the message became as it traveled from child to child.

By the time the message reaches the last person it is rarely in its original form and can even be completely misconstrued. It just goes to show the damage that gossip can do! By the time a story travels around a room, it's seldom in its original form, so imagine what can happen to a story if it travels around an entire school! This is a way to teach kids about gossip and even proper telephone message-taking skills.

Telephone is a great game to play when all the kids are seated around the table in their party hats, munching on cake. Keep those little minds busy!

Chapter
6

Giggle Games

The whole point of kids' games is to entertain the kids, but there's nothing better for an adult than watching the kids laugh. I've done some of my best giggling when I'm hanging out with kids. They know how to have a good time, and the games in this chapter are sure to evoke some side-splitting silliness.

Most of these giggle games can be played by adults, too. They are perfect games for rainy days and snow days. Get the whole family together and be prepared for some good laughs.

Names Of ...

Names of ... is a game you may have played at camp or at club meetings when you were a kid. Your kids are probably well versed in the game and could teach you a thing or two. It's a clapping game that requires a certain amount of hand and brain coordination. I was always terrible at the game because I have no rhythm. It does take a little bit of practice and skill.

All the players sit in a circle with their legs crossed. The more players you have, the better. One person is picked to be the leader and is responsible for setting the rhythm in motion. The rhythm is a slap on thighs, a clap, and two snaps of the fingers (first with the right, then with the left). So the rhythm sounds like this: slap, clap, snap, snap. When everyone is slap-clap-snap-snapping at the same time, the leader thinks of a category and starts when he or she has an idea. Players can speak, one at a time, in turn, on the rhythmic snap of the fingers. Play can go counterclockwise or clockwise—it's up to you.

The play goes like this:

> **Player 1:** Slap, clap … then on the snap, snap: "Names of."
>
> Slap, clap … then on the snap, snap: "Ani-mals" (the word *animals* said to the snapping beat).
>
> **Player 2:** Slap, clap … then on the snap, snap: "Mon-keys."
>
> **Player 3:** Slap, clap … then on the snap, snap: "Ele-phants."
>
> **Player 4:** Slap, clap … then on the snap, snap: "Birds" (note the one syllable— as long as it's said in rhythm, on the snap, you're okay).

As people make mistakes and say a word out of rhythm, or miss a beat and don't say something quickly enough, they are out, and the next person in line picks up the rhythm again.

Names of … is a concentration game, so it's really easy to mess up! I used to mess up because I'd be anticipating my turn and then find myself speechless and laughing when it finally came to me. You have to pick your word and then focus on the rhythm as best you can. The people who go out can stay in the circle and not slap, clap, and snap, snap—or they can leave the circle and the remaining players tighten up the circle.

A few practice rounds of Names of … might be necessary before the game officially begins because it takes a little while to get everyone up to speed. You can make your own rules as you go. You can either change the category whenever a player wants to, or you can make the rule that only the leader is allowed to change the category.

Other fun categories for Names of … are bathroom objects, Chinese food dishes, car parts, types of dogs, countries, and girls' names.

Family Ties

Stuck on what to do for your next family get-together? Don't hesitate to ask your children for suggestions. They probably know more games than you can imagine! You might even want to take turns sharing the responsibility of teaching a new game to family and friends.

That's the Spirit

There is a time for everything, and a season for every activity under heaven: a time to laugh ...

—Ecclesiastes 3:1, 4b

I think God enjoys a good laugh and delights in the giggles of children. I think God understands that families that laugh and play together are forging bonds that will hold them together no matter what the next day brings. If God's Word says there is a time to laugh, then maybe we should make sure we take the time to do it.

Follow the Leader

Two people are selected at the beginning of Follow the Leader—one person to be the leader and another to be the guesser. The guesser must leave the room before the leader is selected. You obviously don't want the guesser to know who the leader is. It's his or her job to figure it out when the game is in motion.

When the guesser is safely outside the room, the leader starts doing goofy things, like scratching an ear, or rubbing his or her nose, or ringing his or her hands. The idea is to do it as surreptitiously as possible so as not to be noticed by the guesser when he or she is called back into the room. The other players must follow the leader. Each time the leader switches an action, the other players must switch to the new action. The players should be as subtle as possible in their transitions also. You want it to be tough for the guesser to figure out who is the leader!

When the play is underway, the guesser is allowed back in the room. It is now the guesser's game! He or she must watch carefully to figure out who the leader is. It could take a few minutes, so you might find a bad case of the giggles beginning as the players wink, wave, and bow around the room. You want to do your best to keep a straight face, but it could be tough! A good leader should be able to graduate to more extreme movements without getting caught—and good players should be able to make the transitions without making the leader an obvious target.

When playing Follow the Leader, don't stand around staring at the leader waiting for the next move—just try to watch him or her out of the corner of your eye somehow. Otherwise, you'll give it away!

Honey, Do You Love Me?

Have the kids form a circle with one child in the center. The child in the center must go up to one of the children in the circle and say, "Honey, do you love me?" The child being addressed must respond, "Honey, I love you, but I just can't smile." If the child being addressed cracks a smile, he or she must go into the center and the child in the center takes his or her place in the circle.

Well, that sounds easy enough—but the trick is that it is the goal of the person in the center to make the person in the circle laugh. The child in the center cannot touch the child in the circle, but can make as many funny faces as he or she wants. You might have to time how long it takes the child to laugh. Usually 30 seconds is more than enough time.

If the child doesn't laugh, the child in the center must do it again to another child in the circle.

With all the giggles this game produces, everyone's a winner!

Sausage

The children sit in a circle with one child standing in the center. The children in the circle may ask the child in the center one question at a time. The questions can be anything the children want to ask. But the child in the circle may only respond by saying "sausage." The first child to make the child in the center laugh, wins—and gets to take his or her place as the sausage-sayer.

For example:

Q: What color is your shirt?

A: Sausage.

Q: What time is it?

A: Sausage.

Q: What is on your head?

A: Sausage.

You can use any word in Sausage—though *sausage* is kind of an amusing one and often gets a few giggles. You can try *rutabaga, rhubarb,* or *pickle.* You can even try changing the word from game to game.

Never Ending Words

The goal of Never Ending Words is to make one long word as a group. Each person takes a turn calling out a letter to add to the previous letter in an effort to make a word. The goal is *not* to be the one to finish the word. Keep adding a letter to try to keep the word going. Eventually it will have to end, but that's the fun part—to see who finally has to put on that closing letter.

For example, player 1 calls out a letter—let's say "c." The player seated either on his right or left (whichever way you decide to rotate play) calls out a second letter (with the intention of building a word—so the second letter should work with the first one). Let's say player 2 calls out "u." Now the word is in the hands of player 3. Let's say he or she calls out "s." As player 4, I might think of the word "custom" and add a "t." However player 5 might be thinking of the word "custard" and will add an "a." The play continues until each player has contributed a letter toward the creation of the word while trying to avoid completing the word.

If you can't think of another letter, you're out and the play continues with the player next to you. You can also try to bluff—add on any letter without a word in mind. Players are allowed to challenge your bluff, however. Only the next person in line to add a letter may challenge the previous player's letter. If you are correct in your challenge, you win the game. If you are incorrect, you're out and the play continues with the next person in line—and the start of a new word!

> **Family Ties**
>
> Small children are not good candidates for Never Ending Words. Their limited vocabularies will frustrate them and turn fun into frowns. Save this game for older kids, and you'll have a much nicer time.

Be careful! If a word is formed along the way in Never Ending Word, the person who forms the word is out.

For instance, if you said D, E, and someone adds N, thinking of DENT, they are out. They formed a word: DEN!

Story Line

This is my favorite imagination game. You can play with as many people as you want, but a good number of people is about 10. Divide into two teams. You will need to do a little preparation in advance—you need a couple index cards that have a crazy sentence written on each one. For example, "The cherry-colored rabbits hopped along the riverbank until they approached the bearded turtle." The goal is to incorporate this crazy sentence into a story line—either at the beginning, the middle, or the end—and see if the other team can guess what the crazy sentence is in the body of the story.

Each team must appoint a spokesperson. The spokesperson reads the card to him- or herself and then shows it to his or her other team members. He or she then begins telling a story.

The spokesperson can, at any time, point to another team member to have that person continue the story where he or she left off. That next person can either continue the story or point to someone else to continue. You can time each person's storytelling (give each person about a minute). Depending on how many people are on a team, the story can be about 10 minutes long. Each person on the team should get a chance to add a portion. Someone should try to get the crazy sentence in before the last person has added to the story line. When the storytelling is finished, the other team has to figure out what the crazy sentence was.

You score points for correct guesses:

- Three points for guessing what the sentence was
- Two points for getting the sentence in
- One point for guessing whether the sentence got in or not

You can also play with both teams contributing to the story. Both teams get a crazy sentence and they both have to fit it into the same story. So you're all telling the same story, but working in a different sentence—you then guess and score in the same way. You can play to 20 points or whatever number you choose.

Chapter 7

Say the Word:
Word Games

There's nothing like word games for getting your kids to learn different ways of seeing and using words. Word games are especially good fun with preteens and teens, as they are learning to flex their intellectual muscles. Imagination and knowledge mean power in the games you'll find in this chapter!

Anagrams

You can play Anagrams with as many players as you want. It's very easy and can even be educational (but don't tell your kids!). Pick a word that has a lot of letters in it and try to make as many words (anagrams) out of that one word as possible. For example:

The word: ESTIMATE

Other words you can make:

time	mate
test	state
meat	meet

... and so on

You should set a time limit on the game, using a timer so there is no debate. There's also nothing like watching the sand slide through an hourglass-shape egg timer to add a little drama to these brain games. When the time is up, players score points for legitimate anagrams. In other words, the anagrams have to be real words that exist in the dictionary—you can't just make up words. You can change the rules from age group to age group. If little kids are involved, let them make two- and three-letter words while older kids have to come up with four- or more letter words.

You score points only if you come up with words that no one else has on his list. If your words match anyone else's words, no one scores points for that word. You have to be really imaginative to score the points—it's hard to see words that no one else will see. Follow these guidelines for scoring:

- Each two-letter word equals one point.
- Each three-letter word equals two points.
- Each four-letter word equals three points.
- Each five-letter word equals four points.
- Each six-letter word equals five points.

Pick a point value to play up to, and whoever reaches the point value first is declared winner.

When playing Anagrams, try to pick a word that has several vowels. This will make it easier for younger players to make words. Also, if you pick a word with a "s" in it, be clear on whether or not you will allow plurals.

Word Bluff

I used to play Word Bluff as a kid in a classroom setting, but you can play it with any group of people—again, the more the merrier.

One person looks up a word in the dictionary and writes it on a piece of paper. It has to be a word you don't think anyone in the room has heard before. Everyone then writes down on a piece of paper what he thinks the word means and puts his name on the paper. All the definitions are then placed into a bag or container of some kind. You can even fold the pieces of paper and put them in the middle of the floor. The person who picked the word also puts a definition into the hat—the real definition, that is!

All the definitions are read out loud by the person who picked the word, and everyone gets to vote for the definition he thinks is correct.

That's the Spirit

Word(s) is used nearly 1,000 times in the Bible. Games that foster a love of words are not only great for building family relationships but also teach children the importance God places on words: "A word aptly spoken is like apples of gold in settings of silver." (Proverbs 25:11)

Each person who guesses correctly scores a point. A point is also given to each person whose wrong definition was believed to be the correct one. If no one guesses the correct definition, the person who originally chose the word gets five points.

The best part about this game is all the crazy false definitions you'll hear. You can make them sound as real or as nutty as you want. But the reader knows the correct definition so he or she will have to read them all out loud with a straight face.

Don't forget to put your name next to the definition so the points can be divvied up at the end of the game. The person who picks the word will also read out the definitions (but not the names of the players written on the paper).

Hangman

I used to play Hangman with my friend at the restaurants with the paper tablecloths—you know the places that supply a few crayons at the table so you can exercise your creative genius while your empty stomach growls. As everyone else drew cartoons, caricatures, and self-portraits, my friend and I played Hangman. He wasn't very good at it. I was only a tiny bit better. It's a fun way to pass the time.

You can play Hangman with more than two people. One player is the person who comes up with the word or phrase while the other players can take turns guessing the letters. It's up to you how you want to set up the game with more than two people.

It may sound kind of gruesome, but the first thing you do is draw the gallows—you've probably seen what they look like in the movies. From the platform going up, draw a straight line and another line perpendicular to the top of that straight line—that's the place your man will hang from when the game is underway.

The rules of the game can vary, but I'll tell you the way I always play.

Think of a word or phrase. You can tell the other player who will be guessing the letters if there's a theme or not—like famous quotes, animal noises, spring flowers, whatever you want. Or you can just pick one word and let the person figure it out.

Next to the scaffolding, draw as many horizontal lines as there are letters in your word or phrase. Let's say you choose the word *daffodil*—you would draw eight horizontal lines to represent the eight letters in the word. These lines are actually blanks—you will fill in the blanks as the guesser comes up with the right letters.

The play begins when your gallows is drawn and your blanks are set.

The person doing the guessing states a letter out loud. If the letter is part of the word or phrase, it is written in the corresponding blank space. If there is more than one of that letter in the phrase, each use must be written into its corresponding blank.

If the letter the person chooses is not in the word, a head is drawn onto the gallows. As you play, you add to your stick man—each arm and leg and a torso. You continue this way until the entire body is drawn. The last thing that should be drawn on the gallows is the noose. Once the noose is drawn, the game is over. The goal is for the guesser to figure out the word or phrase before the picture of the hanging man is completed.

Some people say that you can only draw so many body parts on the diagram before drawing the noose. For example, you can draw the head, torso, arms, legs, and then the noose. If you draw two arms, two legs, the torso, the head, and the noose, you have seven chances to guess it right. That's the hard way to play. I've never played with terribly strict rules. I've allowed eyes, nose, mouth, hands, feet, and even a hat before I drew the noose. I want the guesser to guess the answer—and I'd rather be the hangman drawer than the guesser. That's right—after the other player guesses the word or phrase, the tables turn and *you* are on the guessing side. If the player doesn't get the word in time, you get another chance at controlling the gallows.

To make Hangman more difficult, choose movie titles, book titles, clichés, or well-known phrases for your blanks. The game will go on much longer this way and will be more challenging. For instance, try "Don't count your chickens before they hatch," or "Monkey see, monkey do."

Match Game

Match Game is based on the old television game show of the same name. You can play it at least two different ways. My sisters and I used to play our own home version all the time. We just got pens and pieces of paper and made up our own questions.

You have to divide into two or more teams of an equal number of people. Each team has a captain. You'll also need one leader to ask the questions. This person will be a neutral party like a game show emcee. He or she is not part of either team.

Guess What?

The television game show *Match Game* ran on NBC from 1962 to 1969, and was revived in 1973 as *Match Game PM*. It quickly became the number-one-rated daytime show for the next five years. Gene Rayburn, the host, was nominated for five Daytime Emmys during the game show's time on-air. Panelists often included Richard Dawson, Nipsy Russell, Charles Nelson Reilly, and Brett Sommers. Nowadays, reruns of the show are run on cable and satellite stations.

All the captains stand at the front of the room. Everyone should have a supply of pens and paper before the game begins. The leader asks the group a question and everyone writes down an answer—including the team captains. There is no speaking allowed. Your answer is secret and should not be shown to anyone else. All the pieces of paper are then handed up to the team captains. The team captains read aloud their own answers and then start reading out all the answers from their own teams. You score a point for every answer that matches the team captain's answer.

Family Ties

Word games can be both stimulating and silly. Mom and Dad, have you given yourselves permission to be silly in front of your kids? Letting your children see the sillier side of you makes you seem more approachable. And that will be important in the years ahead.

Here are some sample questions:

If you could have the magical powers of any superhero, who would it be?

If you could live in any city in the world, what city would it be?

What is the greatest movie playing in the theatre right now?

What is the funniest sitcom on TV today?

Another way to play the game is closer to the television show method:

The team captain comes up with a sentence and each player on his or her team has to fill in the blank. For example: "Harriet was at work one day. She looked up from her desk and said 'I am so hungry, I could eat my _____.'" Everyone must fill in the blank. If your answer matches that of your team captain, your team scores a point.

You can set a maximum on the points so that there is an end to the game—15 to 20 points is usually an adequate limit.

Sentence by Sentence

The goal of Sentence by Sentence is to build a complete story by adding a sentence to a series of sentences—but only the preceding sentence is visible. The results are likely to be very silly and often hilarious.

Take a piece of paper and have someone write down a sentence as though beginning a story. The sheet of paper is handed to the next person, who adds a sentence on the line right below the first sentence. Before passing on the piece of paper this time, however, the player must fold down the top of the paper to cover the first sentence. Now only the newly added sentence is showing.

The third player can see only player 2's sentence and must then add another sentence on the line below that sentence. Again, before passing the piece of paper on, player 3 must fold over player 2's sentence so that only his or her sentence is visible. Each time, only the sentence just written will be visible to the next player in line.

The outcome could be something like this:

One day, a limousine pulled up to a house.

The limousine was so long, it took up three parking spots.

The police came to give the driver a ticket.

The driver was so angry he screamed at them.

"No more garbage pick-up for you dirty people."

The streets were teeming with trash.

Disease began to spread.

"An epidemic," cried the local health officials.

No matter what word games you choose to play, your kids' brains will get a workout and the laughs will fly.

They Said What?

While you can use any story, fairy tale, or fable for this game, it's a great way to review Bible stories you and your children are learning. The idea is to fill in the dialog for the people in your story. You don't need to write for this one, so kids of all ages can participate. And the more you encourage players to get into the characters—providing dialogue with feelings like anger, surprise, fear—the more fun it will be for all.

Start out with a two- or three-sentence story-opener that gives the name of a Bible character. For example, start with Moses, David, or Peter. Later on, you can throw in more obscure Bible names (try Miriam, Elisha, Lazarus, or Lydia). It's great fun to see what details the kids remember and to hear the story develop in their own words. Here's an example of how your Bible story might start:

> **Story Starter:** (1 Samuel 17) The Philistines had gathered an army to fight against the Israelites. The Philistine army was camped on one side of a valley and the Israelite army under King Saul was camped on the other side. Every day, the Philistines would send out their champion Goliath, a giant of a man and a fierce warrior. Goliath would stand in the valley facing the Israelites and shout …
>
> **Goliath:** Hey, you guys! Why doesn't somebody come out and fight me? Are you all chicken? I'll make you a deal. Send out your best fighter and if he can kill me, you all go free. But if I kill him, you are all our slaves forever.
>
> When David heard about Goliath's challenge, he said: What's the matter with you guys! I can't believe you're letting him talk that way to you. Don't you know he's making fun of God? You can't let him do that—I'll go fight him myself.
>
> So David went to Saul and said: I'll go fight the giant.
>
> And Saul replied: Are you crazy? You're just a kid and he's one mean dude!

I think you get the idea. Your stories may not be that silly, but they will certainly test your recollection of the story. If you use a Bible version such as the New International Reader's Version, you can actually read the story from the Bible, pausing for the children to fill in the dialogue. After you have concocted aloud your version of the Bible story, reread the real story from the Bible.

Quick on the Draw

While this game isn't really a word game, it is based on the game of Charades. But instead of having people guess a word (or phrase) with miming gestures, they have to guess a word by drawing it. This might sound easy, but it all depends on the word!

This game is a homemade version of the popular board game Pictionary. For this game, you'll need a lot of paper and a couple of pens or pencils. You may also want to use a stopwatch. If you don't have a stopwatch, using a second hand on someone's watch will work.

What you need to do is form two teams. Each team has to think of 12 things that they'd like the opposing team to draw. The things that they think of are written down on 12 separate pieces of paper. The "things" can be anything: objects, sayings, animals, and so on.

Each player on each team takes a turn at drawing one of the items on one of the pieces of paper. The other members of the same team must try to guess what is being drawn. While the players can call out what they think the item is as it is being drawn, the artist cannot say anything to help them along. The artist also may not use any hand gestures or use any numbers or letters in the drawing. Each team is allowed only one minute to draw the picture and figure out what it is.

If the team guesses what the item is before the minute is up, the team scores one point.

To really add to the tension, try an egg timer instead of a second hand. The players will get frantic with the ticking and buzzing as time runs out on their play.

Another team goes next and repeats the same techniques with the same rules.

You'll love to watch everyone's reactions during the game—from the frustrated guessers to the frantic artist. Sometimes crazy arguments break out in the heat of the moment. You'll hear things like "Oh, come on … can't you figure it out?" Or "Oh, come on—where'd you learn to draw?" It's very silly, fun, and action-packed. Even though the artist isn't supposed to speak, sometimes the stress is too much to bear. Each correct guess scores one point, and the team with the most points wins.

Don't get caught without a pencil sharpener. Those fast and furious drawers will go through pencils in no time!

If you are the drawer, make sure you don't say anything. You can't help out the guessers by acting out, saying something, or gesturing to help people along. If you do so, you'll be disqualified.

Chapter 8

Let's Go Team!

Team games are really important for kids to learn and play. They teach kids not only to have a great time with a group of people, but also to learn about strategy, teamwork, and camaraderie. Games like Charades and Up Jenkins teach kids to work together toward a common goal, to listen to their teammates, to come up with good answers, and to use yet another aspect of their creative imaginations.

Many of the games in this book have to do with taking sides, but the games in this chapter are classic team games, many of which have been played for centuries. Charades, for example, is believed to date back to eighteenth-century France. Hide and Seek is even older. There are several variants of these team games as a result of people adapting rules to suit their particular group or geographical location. You'll probably find yourself making up your own rules as you learn to play these games or teach them to your children. One way or another, these games will keep you and your kids busy for hours.

Charades

Charades isn't really considered a game for children. It's often played as an after-dinner entertainment at adult parties. While it started out as a riddle game where participants guessed a word, it eventually evolved into the acting game we are familiar with today.

Guess What?

Charades is believed to have originated in France in the eighteenth century as a riddle game. The goal of the game was to come up with a word or phrase by trying to figure out the riddle. The riddles were given either in prose or in rhyme.

Here is an example:

"My first is a Tartar,
My second a letter;
My all is a country,
No Christmas dish better."

(The answer is Turkey.)

The word version of the Charades game later evolved into an acted game where players had to guess the word or phrase by watching others act them out. That is the version of the game we are most familiar with today.

Charade Parade

Here is what you will need to play Charades:

- A stopwatch or watch with a minute hand to time each charade
- A pen and paper to keep score
- Index cards to write words, sentences, phrases, names of people (your charade cards)
- A neutral player to keep the time and score

Family Ties

Successful families understand and practice teamwork! Learning to be part of a team is an important social skill and an invaluable tool for school activities, adult work life, and successful relationships. It's also part of being a member of God's family. So Mom and Dad, join in the fun and be part of the team!

The point of the game is for players to act out a word, idea, quotation, name of a person, name of a book, movie, or television show in the shortest amount of time possible. Players should split up into two teams.

You should write up the charades on index cards in one of two ways. First, someone can write up the cards in advance. Whoever does this won't be able to play because he'll know the answers. If you choose to write them up before the game, the writer should also be the neutral party that keeps the time and score. That way he or she has a part to play in the game but not in the guessing of the charades.

The other way you can write up charades is to have team one write up the charades for team two and vice versa. That way you ensure that team one and team two will not be acting charades that they already know. Each card can also have a theme written on it—something that will help the teams focus on a certain idea so the guessing doesn't take too long.

To start the game, each team designates a leader. It is the goal of the leader's team to guess the charade that he or she is acting out. The leader cannot use his or her voice in any way and cannot point to any inanimate object in the room as a means to aid the guessers. The secret word or phrase must be completely acted out. The guessing begins the second the acting begins. This is where things can get really rowdy.

The closer the team gets to the answer, and the shorter the time left, you'll find people yelling and waving and laughing their heads off.

Team members can shout out randomly what they think the syllable, word, or sentence is. The other players should also try to listen to the guesses made by other players because every guess could stimulate other ideas—and you don't want to repeat the same guess over and over. When a team member gets something right, the actor can point to that team member and nod, then move on to the next syllable or word.

If the team successfully guesses the answer, the person who comes out with the final word or sentence gets to do the acting, and that team continues play. If the team doesn't guess the answer and time is up, the next team takes the stage with a new word or sentence.

Guess What?

Acted Charades is believed to have originated in England. In fact, William Makepeace Thackeray makes reference to the game of acted Charades in his 1848 novel *Vanity Fair.* The game enjoyed a boost in popularity in the 1930s and then again after World War II. It was a party game then and remains a party game today.

That's the Spirit

Charades takes more skill than many people realize. To make the most of his time, a skillful player will think out his actions before he starts. One bad signal can send teammates on a wild goose chase. The same can be said of our lives in Christ. Our children and the world are watching us—what are our actions telling them about God? "Wise people think before they act; fools don't and even brag about it!" (Proverbs 13:16)

The opposing team is not allowed to shout out any guesses and may not do anything to derail the team doing the guessing. You can play charades in large or small groups. Most commonly it is played by a small group in a living-room setting.

Charades Sign Language

It is important that all players involved know certain hand signals.

- **Movies.** Use one hand to shade your eyes and the other to pretend you're winding the film of a camera—squint one eye as though you're looking through a viewfinder.
- **Book.** Hold your palms together as though in prayer and open and close them as you would a book.
- **TV show.** With your finger in the air, draw an imaginary square in the air. Some people indicate that it's a TV show by pretending to point a remote control.
- **Quote or phrase.** Make quotation marks in the air with your fingers.
- **One finger means first word.** Once everyone says "First word," you can start acting out the word. If no one is getting it, you can act out the first syllable.
- **Syllables.** First indicate how many syllables are in the word by laying the like number of fingers across your forearm—so if the word has two syllables, lay two fingers on your forearm. When everyone says "Two syllables," indicate that you will act out the first syllable first by then laying one finger on your forearm.
- **Length of word.** Make a little or big sign using your two hands (like you're measuring a fish).
- **Sounds like.** Cup one hand behind an ear. This means that you will act out a word that rhymes with the original word.

Some gestures you're just going to have to make up. There are only so many universal gestures you can establish in advance.

Whether you have a neutral party or an egg timer, it's a good idea to establish how long you think each actor should get—usually three minutes is adequate. You don't want to give too much time because that takes the tension out of the play—and too little time might be frustrating for all players involved. You might find you need to play a couple rounds before you figure out the right timing. Act your heart out, as fast as you can, and hope your teammates figure out your waving, bending, hopping, skipping, and grimacing.

Ready, Set, Act!

Establish which team will go first by drawing a name from a hat: team one or team two. The leader of the team that is going to go first pulls one of the index cards from the pile. The card will have a word, sentence, phrase, or person indicated on it (you will have to prepare these cards in advance of the game). The leader of team one then stands at the front of the room, or wherever your designated "stage" is located, and play begins.

Guess What?

There are several versions of charades you can play. One of the funniest I've heard of is Hip Charades. Each team leader spells out a word in the air using— you got it—his or her hips. This game can have some really funny moments.

Once the leader of team one has read the card and takes his or her place, the timekeeper clicks the stopwatch and the team one leader has to start to act—there's no time to waste.

The timekeeper can either be a neutral party (someone not involved in play) or a member of the opposite team who can concentrate on the time and not on the play. Make sure it's someone trustworthy! The timekeeper is responsible for saying "Start" to begin play and "Stop" when the clock runs out.

Score!

There are several different scoring methods you can use.

Each time your team wins a game you score a point. You can play as many rounds as you want. You can set a point limit also—let's say the first team to win 10 points is the winner.

Another way to score is to have the timekeeper record the amount of time it takes to guess the answer. For example, when a team guesses the answer, the time it took them to guess is recorded by the timekeeper (this is why you might need a neutral party). If the answer is not guessed before time is up, three minutes is marked down on the score sheet.

To determine the winner, you add up the times. The team with the lower score is the winner—because it took them the least amount of combined minutes to guess the answers.

Up Jenkins

Up Jenkins is a very silly game that kids just love. It's great for kids' birthday parties or even small adult parties. College kids have been known to play this game late on a Saturday night at the student union, while some adults might have the best time playing the game at home with their kids and their kids' friends. However you play, or whomever you play with, the game is somewhat addictive and is good for an hour or two of good, rowdy fun.

If you decide to play with a group of kids, be prepared for some shrieking because kids really get into it, which makes it all the more fun for the grown-ups. You can play in small or large groups—but you have to sit around a table to play, so play with as many people as you have chairs.

All you need for the game is a coin, a table, and some chairs. Divide the players into two teams. The teams should sit across from each other at the table.

Play starts with everyone's hands under the table. Team one starts the play by passing a coin under the table from hand to hand, back and forth, amongst their own team. It is the goal of team two to figure out where the coin is at a given time. Because the coin is passed under the table, team two can't see where it is as it is passed along. The coin will finally rest with one person. Where it stops nobody knows (at least on team two).

After about 15 seconds the coin passing should stop—it doesn't matter with whom it stops, but you should give it enough time to confuse the opposing team. On a given signal (which your team can agree to before play begins) the coin stops and everyone on team one starts to bang their hands, palms-down—on the tabletop. One person will have the coin and the coin must stay in his or her hand—even as the banging is happening.

Now team two has to guess where the coin is. They do so by pointing to a player and saying "Up Jenkins." Each time a player lifts an empty hand, team two scores a point. Why?—because the object of the game is to leave the palm containing the coin to the very end. If team two guesses the hand containing the coin before the very last hand is revealed, team one scores a point and gets to hide the coin again. If team two chooses all the empty hands and finds the coin in the very last palm, they get a chance to hide the coin.

To save time and chaos, you might want to pick team leaders before Up Jenkins begins. Team leaders can give the signal to stop the coin and start the hand banging, and they can be the ones to call "Up Jenkins."

You'll need to concentrate and keep a very straight face during this game. If you have the coin and you so much as smirk, you could give away the whole game! It's all about the art of the bluff.

Hide and Seek

Hide and Seek is believed to date back to the days of the caveman. Its premise is simple, and it continues to be as much fun for kids today as it was thousands of years ago.

The object of the game is for several people to hide and at least one to seek. Depending on the age of the kids involved, it's not a bad idea to supervise while they play the game. With really little kids, it's essential that you supervise—just in case a kid isn't clear on the rules and isn't sure when to come out of hiding. When I was a kid, one of the kids we played with fell asleep in the hiding place, and we couldn't find him for quite some time!

To play the game, someone is chosen to be "It." To pick "It" check out some of the rhyming games mentioned in Chapter 5. The person who is chosen to be "It" closes his or her eyes and begins to count. Usually the counting occurs at "home base" and goes up to about 50 (or sometimes even 100). Make sure you agree on what number "It" will be counting to before the game begins.

The game starts and ends at home base. It's an important spot because it's the place to where the hiders will run either once they are found or before they are found by "It." Home base is the safe zone.

While "It" is counting, everyone else is trying to find a hiding place. The hiding place should be clever enough so that "It" won't catch the players when he or she starts the search. "It" should be counting loud enough for everyone to hear. If you're doing the hiding, you'll have to listen to where "It" is in the countdown and allow yourself enough time to hide. When "It" reaches the count of 50, or 100, he or she shouts out the number and adds "Ready or not … here I come."

By this point, all the players should be safely tucked away in their own unique hiding spots. The seeker has to go around looking for each player. There are a couple ways you can play this game:

- "It" goes around searching for each player. When he or she spots a hider, he calls out the person's name and the two of them race to home base. If the hider beats "It" to home base, the hider touches home base and says "one, two, three, home free" or "one, two, three for me." That player is considered "safe." If "It" beats the hider to home base, "It" touches home base saying, "One, two, three on Brittney" or "One, two, three on Vincent" (or whatever the name of the person is). The hider is considered "caught."

- The other way to play is to allow the hiders to race home before being found. While "It" is hunting around for hiders, if a hider finds a good moment, he or she is allowed to race home. If "It" sees the hider heading for home, he or she can try to tag that person. If the person is tagged, he or she is caught. If not, that hider is safe.

The first person to be caught in either of these versions of the game is the next "It."

The last person to make it home safely gets to be the next "It." To add a little more fun to Hide and Seek, you can play that all the people who are caught have to help "It" find the rest of the hiders—making the game a little more challenging for the hiders to get home.

Kids will make up all sorts of their own rules as they play the game. There's never just one way to play. But to keep the fights to a minimum, tell your kids to establish the rules round by round.

Sardines

Sardines is Hide and Seek in reverse. All the kids close their eyes and count while one person hides. When the counting is completed (usually to about 25 is fine for this game) all the "Its" must begin the search. When one of the "Its" finds the hider, he or she doesn't say anything but quietly crawls into the hiding spot with the hider. The "It" who finds the player must wait until no one is nearby before crawling into the space with the hider because he or she doesn't want anyone else to find the spot.

Slowly the "Its" will start to disappear and the hiding place will become more and more cramped with hiders. Now you know why the game is called Sardines!

The game ends when the last of the "Its" finds the "sardines." By this point the last "It" will most likely just have to follow the sounds of giggles and squeals. It's not easy to keep quiet when you're all squished, uncomfortably, together.

The first "It" to find the hider gets to be the first hider in the next round.

That's the Spirit

> You both precede and follow me. You place your hand of blessing on my head ... I can never escape from your spirit! I can never get away from your presence!
>
> —Psalm 139:5, 7

God doesn't play hide and seek with us. It should be a comforting thought that we cannot hide from God. He guides and blesses us in the ways of everlasting life. Even when we sin and want to run from him, he pursues us with his love and mercy.

Going on a Picnic: Picnic Games

When the warm weather hits, families often pack up and head out for a picnic. Somehow fried chicken and potato salad just taste better outdoors. Picnics are a great idea for a family fun time. Our family used to gather every summer at my grandparents' house for one full day of picnicking pleasure. It was like a family reunion. Everyone came—aunts, uncles, cousins—all ages and all sizes. It was the one day in the year when we all gathered to talk, eat, and play games.

There are so many games you can play outside, and if you have a big enough family you can get into some really fun competitive activities. But whether your family is big or small, these games will give you hours of giggles.

Many of these picnic games became popular in the pioneer days at country fairs and festivals, but some of the games date back even farther than that. The games in this chapter are old picnic classics that if you've never played before, you'll surely want to play now!

In all likelihood, you will be playing these picnic games with children. Children like to win prizes, so it might be a good idea to have some treats on hand. You can either award little prizes for each race or game, or give a bigger prize to the players or teams that win the most games and races. A pie is a nice prize, or a couple jars of homemade jam—don't forget some candy, fruit, or little toys for the kids. The prize shouldn't be huge, just something fun for the team or players to take home.

Tug of War

All you need for a good game of Tug of War is a long, heavy rope and two teams. This game goes way back to ancient times—it is so simple and so much fun. Draw a line on the ground or place a marker of some kind in the ground. The goal is for both sides to pull on their ends of the rope in order to make the other team cross the line or marker. Some people will use a big mudhole as the line. You know what that means—whoever loses gets covered in mud! I wouldn't recommend that version unless you're by a lake where everyone can dive in when the game is over. You can try putting grease on the rope to make the game a little harder and worth a few more giggles.

You can also play Two-Way Tug of War. Get two heavy ropes and tie them in the middle so that there are four pullable ends. Draw a wide circle on the ground. Divide players into four teams. Each team must stand on the outside of the circle and pull! The first team to be pulled into the circle is out and their end of the rope is left dangling. Now it's a three-way pull. The last team to remain outside the circle is the winner.

> **That's the Spirit**
>
> Our annual family picnic always had tables laden with edible delights of every kind. But what I treasure most from those times is the warm feeling I had knowing that I belonged to so many people. "For the happy heart, life is a continual feast." (Proverbs 15:15)

Off to the Races

Who doesn't remember the fun of a good race? The screaming sideliners, the rush of adrenaline—there's nothing like a good, close race to get the blood pumping and the appetite up. Races also are great for picnics because they take few supplies and have so many variations that you can adapt to almost any number of people or age combinations.

Three-Legged Race

You'll need a start and goal line and several pieces of twine for this game. Form teams of partners. Each player must tie one of his or her legs to the other player's leg so that when they move, they move with three legs. For a Three-Legged Race, you'll want to have a little practice walking around for a while—before the race begins—until you and your partner figure out how to move that leg in unison. It's a lot harder than it looks!

The goal is to race from the start line to the goal line and back again. The first set of partners to reach the start line again is the winner. You can fall and get back up and continue the race, but you won't win unless you catch up to those who are still moving at a steady pace.

Kids will want to pair up with adults in this game, but that might not be good strategy. It is actually easier if the pairs are of similar height and stride. And be careful. You are likely to fall during this race, so try to pick a grassy area for cushion.

Potato on a Spoon Race

For the Potato on a Spoon Race, you'll need some regular-size stainless-steel or plastic spoons and some small- to medium-size potatoes. The potato should be slightly larger than the spoon to make balancing a little tricky. You will also need to establish a start line and a goal line. Everyone balances a potato on his or her spoon and when the whistle blows, he must make it to the goal line and back without dropping his potato. Whoever makes it back first is the winner.

You can also play this game with an egg—but it might be a good idea to hard-boil the egg before the game begins!

Sack Races

For this game, you'll need to dig up some old pillowcases or burlap sacks. Kids really love this game. Each kid climbs into the sack and, holding the edges of the sack up around his or her hips or waist, must hop from the start line to the goal line and back again. Many kids will fall over, and you'll laugh a lot during this crazy game. If adults grab a sack and start hopping with them, the kids will squeal with laughter—the adults will look even sillier than the kids!

A word of warning! Because kids are jumping forward and using their hands to hold the sack, chances are good that when they fall they will land on their faces. A race area that is smooth, flat, and grassy will reduce the "ouch" factor. Also check that there are no sharp stones, sticks, or other kinds of debris hidden in the grass. You might also want to have your kids practice falling in the sack—with a little instruction they can learn to roll as they fall—before they add the speed of racing.

Tag, You're It!

Tag is perhaps the oldest known children's game. You don't need any special tools—just a bunch of kids and an idea. Its premise is simple and the variations exist in the hundreds. For a simple game of Tag, one child is picked as "It" (see Chapter 5 for choosing "It") and all the other children are runners. "It" must try to catch each runner by touching him and yelling "You're It!" In this case, "It" becomes a runner and the tagged runner becomes "It." Here are some of the Tag variations.

Shadow Tag

You have to play Shadow Tag on a sunny day. You can run and run and try to protect yourself from "It," but what you're protecting is not your body, but your shadow on the ground or on a wall. If "It" tags your shadow, you become the next "It."

There are several ways to deal with the people you tag. You can either switch roles so that player becomes "It" and you become a runner, or you can have the tagged player join you as another "It." Then the two of you have to keep tagging other players until everyone is an "It." The first person tagged becomes the next lone "It" for the next game of Tag.

Freeze Tag

In Freeze Tag, when "It" tags a player that person must freeze where he is tagged—that means he freezes in the position in which he was standing when he was tagged. When "It" tags you, "It" yells "Freeze!" So if the person was tagged trying to crawl under a bench, that person must freeze under the bench. If that player was standing on one leg in mid-run, he or she must freeze on that same one leg. He can't move until another free player tags him—then he can "unfreeze" and run again. The game is over when "It" manages to freeze every player. The last person tagged becomes the next "It."

Try this variation: Rather than having to touch a frozen person to unfreeze him, you have to crawl between his or her legs. That can get really tricky—especially if "It" catches you in the act. You'll be frozen in a pretty awkward position.

Touch Tag

This is a great game of Tag for little kids—it's very silly. In Touch Tag, you have to hold the place you were tagged while you run. The person who is "It" in the beginning of the game tries to tag people on a spot on their body that will make it funny or hard for them when they become the next "It." For example: If "It" tags a player on the nose, that person becomes the new "It" and must hold his or her nose while he or she runs and tags other players. Once "It" tags someone else, he or she can let go of his nose and the next player has to be "It" while holding some funny body part.

British Bulldog

This was my favorite Tag game growing up, and we had so many kids in the neighborhood that it was always good fun. One person is "It" and all the other players line up against a wall or some other safe zone. We used to play in the schoolyard, so the school wall was the starting safe zone and the wall across the yard was the other safe zone. The goal was to reach the safe zone before being tagged by "It."

So with all the players lined up against the school wall, "It" must stand midway between the two safe zones (one for each team). When "It" is ready, he or she calls "British Bulldog" and that's the cue for all the kids to start their run toward the opposite safe zone wall. "It" must tag as many players as possible. Whoever he or she tags becomes another "It." When players reach the other wall, they are safe. The kids who were tagged join the original "It" and the next time "British Bulldog" is called, all the "Its" must tag the other players before reaching the safe zone again.

This game gets really fun when there's just one runner left. If that runner somehow miraculously makes it to a safe zone without being caught, he or she is the champ! And there might be days of wild adulation and praise thrown his or her way—to maneuver your way through all those "Its" is a feat of brilliance in the eyes of children. The first person tagged can be the next "It" or you can let the champ be the next "It." Again, make sure everyone is clear on the rules by which you decide to play.

That's the Spirit

Isn't the idea of a safe zone inviting? In our troubled times, we all long to feel safe. Our homes should be a safe zone for every member of the family, and they *can* be when we keep our focus on Christ. "The name of the Lord is a strong fortress; the godly run to him and are safe." (Proverbs 18:10)

You can never run back to the safe zone from which you started! You must run to the safe zone directly across in order to remain safe. It is considered poor sportsmanship in any Tag game to hover around a safe zone. Tag games are about evading and capturing—not hiding!

Capture the Flag

Capture the Flag is another very old game. Kids of all ages love it because it can be quite challenging.

The first thing you need is a big, wide-open space—so this game is perfect for picnics. You should have some wooden marker that you can stick into the ground and also a little flag on a marker that can be stuck in the ground. You can make the flag by tying an old rag to a wooden peg or you can buy little plastic flags from novelty stores.

Divide the field into two boxes. You can do this by bringing wooden pegs to push into the ground that mark out the playing area (tent stakes are great). At the back of each playing box in the far left corner is a "jail"—you can mark this out with more wooden pegs as well. One person on each team acts as a jailer and stands in front of the jail box. The flag should be located to the right of the jail right behind the place where the goalie will stand. The goalie should stand to the right of the jail and the flag (about 10 feet away). The rest of the teams stand behind the boundary line that divides the two territories. Once a team member steps into the opposing team's territory, he or she can be tagged.

Obviously, the object of the game is to capture your opponents' flag by entering their territory. You must do so without getting tagged, tackled, or otherwise mangled! This game gets very rowdy, so you might want to wear a few layers of protective clothing!

When the game begins and players start running into the opposition's territory, it is the job of the other teammates to capture the opposing team's players. If you are tagged, you are sent to jail and must stand in the marked jail area at the back of the opposition's territory. You can only be freed from jail if one of your own teammates makes it that far into the territory and is able to tag you. If that happens, you don't have to dash about trying not to get caught—rather, you get a free walk back to your own territory without being tackled.

It is not easy to capture the flag, especially with that goalie hovering around it. The trick to the game is to have a strategy worked out with your teammates before the game begins. You will have to find a way to distract the goalie so you can capture the flag and run it back into your own territory.

Teenagers and adults enjoy playing Capture the Flag at night. It's especially perfect when there is a lot of moonlight. If you choose to play the night-time version, make sure that the area of play is secure and that everyone has working flashlights.

Leap Frog

I've seen everyone from little kids to 30-year-olds play the game of Leap Frog. Adults look really silly playing the game, and many of us with lower back pain should be careful about indulging in this popular activity too often. But if you're up for it, give it a whirl—especially with little kids. They'll laugh their heads off trying to climb over an adult's back.

To play the game, everyone bends over in a line. The last child in the line jumps over all the bent-over backs, one after the other—by placing his or her hands on the flat of the back and lifting his body over. He or she keeps doing this until he reaches the front of the line and bends over for the next round. The last child again stands up and leaps over the other players ahead of him again—until he reaches the front of the line. This is a slow way to move forward, but you'll never have so much fun getting someplace.

Guess What?

Leap Frog has been around for centuries. In fact, there is a reference to the game in a children's book dating back to 1744 called *Little Pretty Pocket Book*.

To help the little kids, an adult can duck down all the way onto the ground by getting down on his knees and tucking his head under (called making a *low back*). Little kids with little legs will have an easier time leaping over you that way.

You can play the game with as few as two people and as many as you can find to play. Two kids can play the game—leaping over each other on their way across the park. They're bound to be dizzy by the time they reach their destination, however!

Plain and Simple

A **low back** is a term used in Leap Frog for getting down on your knees, tucking your head under, and making yourself as small as possible—a good position to be in for little leapers. A **high back** is bending over and holding your ankles or knees, making yourself higher than a low back, and making your position more challenging for the leaper.

Frisbee Games

The history of the Frisbee is perhaps more interesting than the game itself. It's a true American product that came into popularity out of poverty and ingenuity. In the late nineteenth century and well into the twentieth century, children used to play with metal cookie tin and pie tin lids by tossing them to each other in a kind of game of catch. It is rumored that the most commonly tossed tin lid was that of an American company called the Frisbie Pie Company, which is how the Frisbee got its name. The Frisbie lids were especially popular on college campuses. The sport of tossing pie tin lids grew during the Great Depression years, and soldiers took the practice overseas during World War II.

The problem with the tin lid was that it didn't glide very easily and it made a horrible shrill noise when it flew threw the air. It also hurt to catch one. Sometimes the lids would crack or break and then the edges became sharp and dangerous.

So after the war, two veterans—Walter Morrison and Warren Franscioni—took it upon themselves to manufacture a kinder, gentler Frisbee. They manufactured a better flying disc, but it still had some major flaws due mainly to primitive plastic materials. Morrison later developed a better flying disc and called it the Pluto Platter—named after the planet Pluto—which looked like a flying saucer. When two small toy company owners met up with Morrison, they offered to perfect and mass manufacture his product. They struck up a deal and took the product to college campuses. Students at Harvard were thrilled by the invention because, as they admitted, they'd been playing with the tin lids from the Frisbie Pie Company for ages. So the small toy company called "Wham-O" named the flying disc "Frisbee"—changing just one letter in the spelling—and the life of the Frisbee came full circle.

Most picnic-goers will bring along a Frisbee and use it just for fun—tossing it back and forth and catching it—with no heavy-duty competition involved. You need a wide-open space, and make sure you're not too close to other picnic-goers. Frisbees have a tendency to fly a little erratically on a windy day, and you don't want anyone to get hurt. If you get tired of tossing the flying disc back and forth aimlessly, give Ultimate Frisbee a shot.

Ultimate Frisbee

Frisbee has become a very popular game in many countries of the world. Ultimate Frisbee is probably the most popular and most competitive version of Frisbee out there today.

To play the game, you need seven players on each side and a large field at least half the size of a football field. You also need markers to mark the end zones at either end of the field. You will find that this game is similar to football, only it is played with a Frisbee. The major difference is that a player can never run with the Frisbee—it must always be in motion.

The regulation field is 70 yards by 40 yards with end zones 25 yards deep.

Both teams line up in front of their own end zone lines. You can flip a coin to determine who tosses the Frisbee first. The team that tosses is the defense and the receiving team is the offense. To start play, the defense throws the Frisbee to the offense. It is now the job of the offense to throw the Frisbee past the end zone of the defense. The defense must intercept the toss. Each time the offense is successful, they score a point. If the offense is intercepted, the play transfers to the defense and the roles are reversed: The defense becomes the offense and the offense becomes the defense.

The disc can be tossed to a teammate before an attempt to toss it across the end zone is made. The teammates can run and toss to try to get closer to the opponent's end zone. The Frisbee must always be in motion; a player cannot hold it for longer than 10 seconds and can never run with it in hand.

You can assign each player to be a "marker" when you are on the defensive team. Each marker is assigned to a thrower. As a marker you should attempt to block the thrower from making a successful toss without touching him or her—touching constitutes a foul. The marker is also responsible for counting, to make sure the thrower doesn't hold the Frisbee for more than 10 seconds. If a toss is not completed, the teams switch offensive and defensive roles.

Horseshoes

Horseshoe pitching is another very old game—dating back to pioneer times and beyond. It is believed that the game was started by blacksmiths because they are the ones who would have had several extra horseshoes lying around.

The horseshoes used in these games are very heavy—heavier than the actual shoes put on the horses—so be careful if little children are around. They shouldn't be too close to the playing area because they could get hurt when the shoes start flying. You can buy plastic sets for children to use. They are very inexpensive and can be picked up at almost any toy store. The adult kits can also be purchased at sporting goods stores and can range quite a bit in price.

There are some people who play the game very seriously, and there are official rules—but if you're playing at home, just divvy out the horseshoes and start tossing them at the stake. You'll find the challenge of getting the horseshoe around the stake competition enough when you first get started. Those horseshoes are pretty heavy, and you'll be surprised how hard it is to predict where they will land after being tossed.

> **Family Ties**
>
> Games like Horse-shoes are a great way to get different generations interacting. Although Grandma and Grandpa might not be up for a sack race or tag, they might enjoy teaching your youngsters the finer points of horseshoe tossing. And don't forget to take lots of pictures to preserve those precious moments.

If you want to make the game a little more competitive, try these rules, which are loosely based on the NHPA official rules (National Horseshoe Pitchers Association of America).

You should have several feet of playing area—at least 50 feet. Two stakes should be placed at either end of the field—at least 40 feet apart. You can play on any surface: grass, gravel, or pavement. Just remember: The harder the pavement, the louder the game. Those horseshoes can really clatter when they strike the ground. You should mark a foul line about three feet in front of each stake. This means you have to throw past the foul line in order for the pitch to be good. This will make your throwing distance 37 feet—you should throw all the way from the opposite stake on the other side of the field.

Each player or team gets two horseshoes. The teams stand at opposite sides of the field and take turns pitching their shoes. The teams alternate throwing the two shoes. Player one throws his or her two shoes, then player two throws his or her two shoes. Each throws from behind his own foul line toward the stake at the other end of the field.

A shoe must fall within one horseshoe width to be considered for points. A horseshoe width is the distance between the two sides on the open end of the shoe. The closest shoe to the stake scores one point. If two of your shoes are closer to the stake than any of your opponent's shoes, you score two points. Horseshoes that completely encircle the stake ("ringers") score three points. If you have the closest shoe and it's a ringer, you score four points. If your opponent throws a ringer on top of yours, neither one of you scores any points. If your shoe rests leaning on the stake (a "leaner"), you score a point and it is considered the closest shoe next to a ringer.

You keep playing the game until someone scores 40 points.

Plan your family picnic with enough time so no one has to feel rushed. Part of what makes a picnic so wonderful is that it allows plenty of time for play and relaxation. Don't forget the ants!

Guess What?

An average horseshoe weighs about 2 pounds, 10 ounces. That might not sound like a lot, but it feels pretty heavy when you have to toss it.

Part

2

Holiday Happenings

Holiday celebrations are the source of many rich family traditions and lasting family memories. As you ponder the heritage you are creating for your children, traditions will no doubt play an important role in establishing meaningful memories for your family. For each holiday, there are ideas for crafts that can be used to decorate your home or as gifts for family and friends. There's even a recipe or two provided to add to the holiday festivities.

Holidays like Christmas, Thanksgiving, and Easter are also sacred opportunities to teach children about God and your faith. While you work together on the crafts and recipes, you can also share your memories of holidays past. You can talk with them about what each holiday means to you and how it has contributed to your faith. As you consider how your family will choose to celebrate holidays throughout the year, you can use the creative ideas here to build warm and lasting family traditions.

Chapter 10

Creating Family Traditions

tra•di•tion (*truh-DISH-uhn*): noun. The handing down of customs, ideas, and beliefs from one generation to the next. A custom, idea, or belief that is handed down in this way.

Traditions practiced according to our cultural heritage help us to establish our identity within the groups we call family, extending far and wide and sometimes to other countries we have never visited ourselves. Traditions often are the ties that will bind us even if we have little else in common. They let us know we belong.

But traditions are also about beliefs. Traditions practiced in our Christian faith help us grow spiritually and maintain hope. They also help us develop discipline. Family traditions that center around shared values and beliefs give us something to hang on to in times of doubt. They are not the true essence of faith, but they help us be faithful.

Family traditions don't have to be complicated, and they can take many forms, but the more they connect to our senses, the more lasting the memories they create. Sounds, smells, tastes, and touch—simple acts that incorporate these in ways that excite our emotions and warm our hearts and are often repeated will long be remembered.

Traditions from the Kitchen

My grandmother, Geraldine Wellsby, was truly a creator of family tradition. She made sure that our family—including all the aunts, uncles, and cousins—got together several times a year. We all shared Thanksgiving dinner, and the day after Thanksgiving Grandma started baking cookies for our annual Christmas Eve get-together. She baked every grandchild their favorite cake for his or her birthday (mine was fudge swirl with mocha icing), and she passed on to our family dozens of recipes that evoke warm memories of the value of family.

Traditions from the kitchen appeal to so many of our senses—and they are passed on and maintained (even though they sometimes morph a bit) because they represent a connectedness, a relationship, we all long for and need.

Some family traditions have deep meaning and have been passed down through generations. But they needn't all be so rich with meaning. Simple, repeated family fun can be just as significant. Here are a few ideas.

Pizza night: Letting the children add their own toppings increases the fun. Buy a plain frozen pizza from the store or one of the take-home-and-bake variety and have everyone's favorite toppings available. You can divide larger pizzas into sections for family members to top off as they please, or try small individual pizzas—one for everyone. Once in a while make everything from scratch. Add a game or a movie to the evening, and a traditional family night is born. Not only does this have the potential to become a consistent tradition, but it also stops the world for an evening for fellowship with just the family members. When the kids are teens, it can help keep them grounded in the family community.

Waffle day: One family established this on Saturday morning and another on Sunday. It's those rarest of times when Dad cooks. Whether he turns up waffles or flips out pancakes, kids love seeing Dad being "creative" in the kitchen. The kids kick in their own creativity with toppings. The sky is the limit: syrup, jam, whipped cream, pie filling, nuts, or sliced fruit—any or all can end up on top (the only caveat being that what you create, you have to eat). And Dad cleans up! Moms, that's part of the tradition you will want to preserve for years and years and years. Good for Dad!

A missionary friend who has always lived far away from her granddaughter developed a beautiful plan for making their rare visits memorable. Whenever she arrived on furlough, she brought along a carefully selected demitasse cup. The first thing she would do was to sit down with her little (and later, not-so-little) granddaughter and have a tea party. She would bring goodies to share, leaving the cup behind as a reminder of her love. This precious time spent together was their reintroduction each and every time. When the collection of cups had grown too large, she began to bring tiny spoons and assorted utensils for tea time.

All traditions start out new at some time, so don't hesitate to start one of your own. A few years ago I found a wonderful recipe for homemade peanut butter dog biscuits. Now every year at Christmas, my girls and I roll and cut out these treats for Brittany, our Springer Spaniel. She loves eating her angel, star, and tree-shape good-ies, and we always roll with laughter when she bites the head off her "gingerbread" man. Not a very "traditional" tradition, but maybe that's the point!

What a Tradition Might Sound Like

Familiar sounds can also become part of family traditions. Music plays an important part in many holiday celebrations, so there are pieces of music and certain song lyrics that have become interwoven in our collective family memories. Here are some ideas for using sound to create traditions in your family:

 Family Ties

With the move toward contemporary worship in many of our churches, many beautiful hymns are not making their way into the next genera-tion. Why not take on the family project of choosing a hymn for your family? You could research the ori-gins, talk with Grandma and Grandpa about their favorites, and then learn to sing it together.

- Have a special rhyme or song you sing at bedtime every night with your children. I have a little rhyme I started when my girls were very young. Now that they are in their early teens, I still sneak it in every now and then. They protest, of course! But the grins on their faces tell me that they appreciate being reminded of our history together.

- Christmas carols are a wonderful family tradition. Many families make it a point to gather around the piano each year to share in a few of their favorite Christmas songs. What a great way to internalize the truths of the faith!

- Singing a short chorus of thanks at mealtime instead of saying grace is another great way to add the gift of remembered sounds to family times.

- Not all family traditions with sound have to involve music. How about a favorite poem or Bible verse becoming part of your family celebrations? Family blessings have a strong history in Scripture, especially among the Israelites. A family blessing pronounced by the oldest family member present at your family gatherings could prove to be a keeper for generations to come.

Traditions of Celebration

Into the life of every family comes those special times of celebration commemorating milestones reached by individuals in the clan. Family celebrations are a perfect time to pass along family traditions or to start new ones.

Birthdays

Not every culture celebrates birthdays the same way. In fact, in many European countries people celebrate the date of the death of their patron saint instead of the date of their own birth. Even in those places where one's birth is celebrated, it can be done in different ways. Some celebrate on the exact moment of birth, even if it happens to be 2:17 in the morning! Some families combine birthdays into one large family celebration day.

Whatever the tradition in other countries, we tend in our culture to consider the anniversary of a person's birth an excellent occasion for revelry. Children love the attention—as do most adults, although some "grown-ups" don't care to be reminded that all those candles on the cake represent more than a fire hazard!

As complicated as it can get sometimes, don't let this important tradition slip by. Every birthday is an occasion to remind everyone in your family that without the birth of that individual, your family would not be as precious as it is today. That day of birth has been thought of by God for all eternity and he or she is precious in his sight. So light the candles, cut the cake, receive thoughtful gifts, and sing your family's version of a favorite song on the subject.

> **That's the Spirit**
>
> Here's a blessing from Scripture you might consider adopting for your family:
>
> May the Lord bless you and protect you. May the Lord smile on you and be gracious to you. May the Lord show you his favor and give you his peace.
>
> —Numbers 6:24–26

Guess What?

Some birthday traditions have interesting roots. For example, you can thank the ancient Greeks for the custom of having a birthday cake, although they might have borrowed the idea from the Persians. The Greek birthday cake, in honor of the goddess of the moon, Artemis, was round and often decorated with candles. The candles may have been used to symbolize light and life.

Thanksgiving

Even when family gatherings are sometimes complicated, no one wants to be alone on this very family-centered day. For that reason, some families traditionally have extended their family gathering to include people outside the family who might otherwise be alone, making them honorary family members. As with Christmas and Easter, the focus should be on gratefulness for God's gifts to us.

There are variations on the details of such holiday celebrations, sometimes influenced by cultural traditions (which add that much more to the occasion). And the house is never really too small. Here are a few of my family's Thanksgiving traditions to get you thinking:

- It's Dad who stuffs the bird! Even if it means getting up at 3 or 4 A.M.! I still remember the first year I got up early enough to see the cooked giblets being sliced and diced. What an impression that little lesson in turkey anatomy made on me!

- Watching the Macy's Thanksgiving Day parade on TV. I remember doing this with my mom and now my daughter watches with me. It's a real generation-bridger.

- Football! Whether you play a family version of touch football or cheer on your favorite team, if you want to include the men in your family, this is an important tradition to observe.

- After dinnertime, we play card games, board games, and Twister. We take walks (and some take naps!) and we talk together more on that one day than we do in any combination of other days.

- We practice serving others! This has taken many forms over the years—sometimes we participate in collecting food for the needy or serving a meal to the homeless. Other times, it's an attitude of service to each other that we cultivate at home—clearing someone else's place at the table, helping with dishes, playing a game someone else wants to play even if we don't.

As the celebration of Thanksgiving reminds us to gather together and count our many blessings, we can be a living demonstration to others that "family" is one of God's greatest blessings.

Christmas

Christmas is another time steeped in traditions and full of religious significance. There are so many wonderful opportunities during this celebration to reinforce true values in our children.

There are many Christmas traditions that you can carry on or begin for your family. The following are some classics that you might consider:

Family Ties

Interviewing members of your extended family about holiday traditions can be a rewarding walk down memory lane. Or make it an assignment for family members. It can be done with a visit or a phone call or a request sent in the mail. The information you gather can then be shared with other family members—perhaps at a family reunion or in a family newsletter.

- Reading the Christmas story (Luke 2:1–20; Matthew 2:7–12) as a family is especially meaningful. Making it an honor that is shared—starting with the oldest and passing it down each year—helps this tradition last.

- Light Advent candles, one each Sunday in December, in anticipation of Christmas. Talk together about how as a family you can prepare your hearts and home for the coming celebration of Jesus' birth.

- Collect storybooks about Christmas that you read together every year, maybe one each night from December 1 through December 24. Include books about different Christmas symbols and traditions you can learn about together—the tree, certain songs, the candy cane, St. Nicholas, wreaths. You might discover a new tradition you want to adopt.

- Make trimming the tree a time to remember. Start a collection of ornaments with special significance for each child in the family. There was once a young couple who began their marriage decorating their Christmas tree with all they had at the time: bits of red ribbon tied in little bows. As children entered into the family, Mom and Dad began adding an ornament each year for each child. When the time came for that child to leave home, his or her ornaments were sent along to start a new family tree. Finally the Christmas came when the last child had left home, and the tree had only the red ribbons. But rather than find it sad, the couple remembered the love they had shared in those first years of their marriage, and they joyfully began to anticipate new traditions yet to be started.

Commit to Family Traditions

Whether it is preserving old traditions or creating new ones, our families need traditions. Traditions help to define our memories. Traditions link generations past and future together and help us teach values to our children.

The Ties That Bind

Take time to evaluate your family's traditions. What more can you do to preserve your family's history through traditions? What new traditions can you create to ensure that your children have valuable and lasting memories? Be purposeful about it. What will the children remember? What will they look forward to?

Talk with your extended family—Mom, Dad, siblings, grandparents, aunts, uncles—to rediscover meaningful traditions from your past. In America we have become so mobile that we have lost our connections to much of our family history. We tend to dwell on opposite sides of the country instead of the other side of town. And there is a stability that is lost for us. Families help each other. Maybe there are some traditions that we need to revive.

Perhaps the greatest family "tradition" is family devotions in the evening. Every member doesn't have to be there and the devotions don't have to be long or complicated, but they will allow God to bless your family in very special ways.

Single-Parent Families Need Traditions ...

Single-parent families have a particularly rough road. God's intent from the beginning has been that children be raised with a mom and a dad in the home. But in this broken world, this cannot always be the reality. The holiday season often brings the pain of loss again and again to the surface. If you are such a parent, you will need all the more to be purposeful about traditions.

You can invent traditions the children can carry from home to home, while others you will want to make unique to your home. Try to maintain a few traditions from the time before death or divorce made you a single parent. These past traditions give important continuity to the holidays for your children and remind them that they still belong. But if some traditions create memories that are too painful for you to deal with right now, that's okay. Put them aside for a time but leave the door open to revisiting them another year, and take your cue from your kids as to what traditions are important to their healing.

But new traditions are important, too—so that you and your children can look forward to your new life together. Here are a few suggestions of new traditions you might try:

- Go to an early church service on Christmas Eve and come home to sandwiches or pizza. Stay up late and open your presents at midnight. Then you can sleep in on Christmas Day—a real treat for most single parents.

- Give fewer gifts. This might be a financial necessity. But you can attach it to a new family tradition. Give your children all the flyers and catalogs that arrive in your home. Let them go through and mark the items they want—creating a wish list—with the clear understanding that they will only get a certain number (two or three) of the things they mark. They should also choose one gift to give to a needy child.

- Celebrate Christmas on a different date. If your children will not be with you for Christmas, pick a new day for your family celebration. Or use the pattern of the Jewish Hanukkah—celebrate over a period of several days. Whatever you do, don't stay home alone. Go visit family or friends and participate whole-heartedly in their family celebrations.

The holidays can be an especially difficult time for single parents. But keep in mind that you are still a family and traditions old and new can help you and your children to find a new life together.

 That's the Spirit

> A family should maintain a variety of traditions that give each member a sense of identity and belonging.
> —James Dobson

Traditions are precious riches and provide a sense of belonging beyond value—fill your home with them! "A house is built by wisdom and becomes strong through good sense. Through knowledge its rooms are filled with all sorts of precious riches and valuables." (Proverbs 24:4)

Some Additional Tradition-Building Ideas

The Mad Hatter in Disney's *Alice in Wonderland* sings "Statistics prove, prove that you've one birthday, one birthday ev'ry year. But there are 364 unbirthdays. That is why we're gathered here to cheer." If you add in all the other familiar holidays, you still have more than 350 "un-holiday" days to celebrate! Here are a few ideas on how to start family traditions for some of those other days:

- Leaf-raking festival day: Everyone in the family participates, anticipating hot cocoa or another family favorite delight upon completion. Incorporate an elderly neighbor's yard while you're at it. Then invite him or her to the reward celebration.

- Have a cookie-baking jubilee or a cookie exchange with another family. This is especially helpful during those hectic pre-Christmas daze—I mean days!

- Let every family member celebrate one un-birthday on a day of his or her choosing. The only requirement is that they make their choice known to the family at least 10 days in advance. Wrap up stuff from around the house that you know the unbirthday person will enjoy, even if it has to be returned to the owner at some designated time. A favorite meal, the exchange of kind words, and you have a wonderful family celebration!

- Watch a certain movie only once a year. When I was a child they ran *The Wizard of Oz* on television once a year. It was a family tradition that we all gathered to watch it, even though it was many, many years before I was old enough to stay awake until the very end. Some other suggestions: *Meet Me in St. Louis* with Judy Garland traces a Victorian-era family through the four seasons (and celebrations) of a year. *It's a Wonderful Life* with Jimmy Stewart is a perfect Christmas tale full of Christian family values.

- Gather sometime after Christmas and have a thank you note-writing session. Make them simple or make them unique. Just make sure they are sent (note to self!). Help children to learn this fading art of expressing appreciation.

Chapter 11

Heartwarming Valentines

Valentine's Day is often associated with romantic love. But the fullest meaning of love is found in the Bible. The entire thirteenth chapter of 1 Corinthians defines it. Here's a sample, but read the entire chapter for yourself:

> Love is always patient and kind; it is never jealous; love is never boastful or conceited; it is never rude or selfish; it does not take offense, and it is not resentful.
>
> —1 Corinthians 13:4–6

This biblical statement of love encompasses the heart and soul of Valentine's Day. It's a time when people remember their loved ones with flowers, cards, gifts, and other expressions of their affection. Sweethearts are taken out to dinner, and in many cases marriage is proposed. It's a great time to gather family and friends together and tell them what we should be telling them all year long—"I love you!"

But where and how did this special day originate? Some experts say that Valentine's Day was based on the ancient Roman festival—Lupercalia—which was celebrated on the eve and day of February 15. This festival was dedicated to courtship, good crops, and mating. It was the custom for the men in the village to strike people with animal hides to ensure their fertility. After the arrival of Christianity, in many areas this festival was replaced with a Christian celebration, based on the life of St. Valentine. Many scholars believe that there were several martyrs named St. Valentine whose feast days were held on February 14. It is unsure, however, if there was any connection between them and the Valentine's Day custom of love and courtship.

Nowadays, to celebrate Valentine's Day is to open your heart to love and enjoy a relaxing day with your family and friends. It's a perfect holiday to make a special craft for a loved one or to just spend some time together eating chocolates and having fun.

Family Ties

As parents, the most important gift we can give our children is love. It helps them know their worth and the God who created them. But are you expressing love in a way your child understands? It might be quality time, words of affirmation, gifts, acts of service, or physical touch. In their book *The Five Love Languages of Children*, Gary Chapman and Ross Campbell, M.D., explain how to effectively communicate love to our children in a way they can best understand it. I highly recommend it!

Counting the Ways of Love

How do I love thee? Let me count the ways …. You can express your love for your family and friends by making them a symbol of your affection. Check out this section for great ideas for gifts of love for every member of your family.

Guess What?

Did you ever wonder where the tradition of giving Valentine's Day cards originated? One theory is that they were a result of a Roman lottery that was held in honor of the god Lupercus during the festival of Lupercalia. In this lottery, the names of willing young women were placed in a box and picked out by young men. The matched pair would share companionship during the year. Pope Gelasius outlawed the pagan festival of Lupercalia and created a Christian festival based on the life of Saint Valentine. He replaced the old lottery with a new lottery that celebrated the lives of the saints. In this lottery the names of saints were placed in a box. Both men and women picked a saint that they were expected to emulate during the year. Many men were unhappy with this new arrangement and, instead, sent letters of affection to the women they wished to court. These greetings are thought to be the first Valentine's Day cards.

Love Letters

It just wouldn't be Valentine's Day without Valentine's Day cards. Remember when you were little and stuffed your Valentine's Day cards for your classmates into a big decorated box? When they were passed out, there was usually one that stood out in the mass of greetings—that special homemade card. Recreate this memory by making your own personalized cards for your loved ones.

Level: Easy

Time involved: Half to one hour

Materials:

> Card stock
>
> Pack of foam letters
>
> Glue gun
>
> Pack of foam hearts
>
> Piece of jewelry wire
>
> Calligraphy marker

1. Fold the card stock in half to make a card with the fold at the top. Spell out the word "Valentine …" with the foam letters, and glue them onto the front of the card.

2. Glue large foam hearts onto each side of the word "Valentine …." Glue smaller hearts of another color on top of the first hearts and even smaller hearts of another color on top of the second hearts. You can also use any design of hearts you choose.

3. Allow the hearts to dry. Meanwhile, make a tiny spring out of the jewelry wire by twisting a four-inch piece of wire into a spiral. Glue together the same order of hearts as on the front of the card. Glue these to the spiral. Glue the spiral of hearts onto the inside of the card. When the recipient opens the card, the hearts will spring out at him or her.

With a calligraphy marker, write "You make my heart leap!" on the inside of the card.

That's the Spirit

Would you like to read a love letter to you? The Bible is God's love letter to you and your family. And because God is love (1 John 4:8), he knows just what to say. Check out this verse on God's love for you:

> For the Lord your God has arrived to live among you. He is a mighty savior. He will rejoice over you with great gladness. With his love, he will calm all your fears. He will exult over you by singing a happy song.
>
> —Zephaniah 3:17

Checkers Anyone?

Play a quiet game of checkers with your Valentine using these unique heart-shape pieces and checkerboard. The fun part is collecting your rewards when you capture your opponent's pieces.

Level: Moderately easy

Time involved: Two to three hours, including drying time

Materials:

> Newspaper or plastic
>
> 24 (1-inch) wood hearts
>
> Red and white craft paints
>
> Paintbrushes
>
> Black fine-tip marker
>
> Clear acrylic finish spray
>
> Checkerboard

1. Place a layer of newspaper or plastic on your work area to protect it. Paint 12 hearts with red paint and 12 hearts with white paint and allow them to dry.

2. Using the marker, write a favor on one side of each piece, such as a back rub, a kiss, a hug, a special treat, or a piece of candy. Once a checker is captured, it can be redeemed for that prize. Spray the checkers with clear acrylic finish spray and allow them to dry.

If you don't want to bother with paints but would like to play this game of favors, try using pre-cut heart-shape foam pieces as the checker pieces.

You might want to make your own checkerboard out of 12 × 6 inch square red-and-white foam sheets and a 12-inch square piece of cardboard. Mark off eight 1½-inch spaces across the top and bottom of the white foam sheet. Mark off four 1½ inch spaces along the sides of the foam sheet. Using a ruler, draw the vertical lines matching up the 1½ inch marks. Draw horizontal lines matching up the 1½ inch marks along the sides, making 32 (1½-inch) squares. Repeat this step using the red foam sheet. Cut out 32 (1½-inch) red squares and 32 (1½-inch) white squares. Glue the squares onto the cardboard, alternating colors. You should have eight squares across and eight squares down the board. The squares should completely cover the cardboard.

A Hearty Welcome

Welcome visitors to your home with this lovely heart-shape slate sign. You can put this out for Valentine's Day or make other signs with your kids' names on them to hang on their bedroom doors.

A welcoming sign for visitors to your home.

Level: Moderately easy

Time involved: One to two hours

Materials:

Transfer or carbon paper

Scissors

Heart-shape slate (This can be found in craft stores in the slate section.)

Masking tape

Copy paper or tracing paper

Pen

Pink, red, brown, black, and white craft paints

Paintbrushes

Foam plate

Clear acrylic finish spray

Guess What?

Roses are a symbol of Valentine's Day. In ancient times roses symbolized peace and war as well as love and forgiveness. The type of roses you send to a loved one can have a hidden meaning. Red roses symbolize passion, white roses are for true love and innocence, yellow roses mean friendship, and black roses symbolize farewell.

1. Cut a piece of transfer or carbon paper to fit the heart-shape slate. Tape this to the slate. Using copy or tracing paper, trace the following Valentine design. Place the copy or tracing paper on top of the transfer paper and tape it in place. Using a pen and moderate pressure, trace over the design to transfer it to the slate. Remove the copy paper and transfer paper from the slate.

2. Paint the design in with the appropriately colored craft paints. Paint the bear brown with a black nose and the hearts pink or white. Allow the slate to dry.

3. Spray the slate with clear acrylic finish spray and allow it to dry.

Sample design for a Valentine's Day welcome.

(Melissa LeBon)

Scent-Sational Soaps

Making homemade soaps is easier than you might think. You can make these heart-shape soaps to decorate your bathroom or give them to your loved ones as gifts.

Level: Moderately easy

Time involved: Two to three hours, plus overnight to harden

Materials:

> Glycerin block
>
> Knife
>
> Microwave-safe disposable cup
>
> Soap scent
>
> Red and white soap dye
>
> Craft stick or old spoon
>
> Heart-shape soap molds
>
> Bag of white soap chips
>
> Toothpick
>
> Bag of red soap chips
>
> Soap dish

1. Cut off two squares of the glycerin block and place them in a microwave-safe cup. Microwave this on high for 40 seconds, or according to manufacturer's directions, until melted. Add two drops soap scent and one drop red dye to the mixture. Stir the mixture with a craft stick or old spoon.

   You can avoid the hassle of collecting all the ingredients necessary for soap making by buying a kit that contains the materials, the molds, and the directions. That way you can see if you enjoy the craft before investing a lot of money in the individual products.

2. Pour the mixture into the heart-shape mold. Add a few white soap chips to the mixture and stir. Use a toothpick to poke any bubbles that may occur and refill if necessary.

3. Repeat this step using red and white dye to make pink soap and then again using only white dye and red soap chips. You should have approximately two heart soaps that are red with white chips, two that are white with red chips, and two that are pink.

4. Allow the soaps to harden overnight. Remove the soaps from the molds and place them in the soap dish.

Heart to Heart

This simple Valentine's Day wreath would make an elegant decoration for your home or a perfect gift for a friend or relative.

Level: Moderately easy

Time involved: One to two hours

Materials:

>   25-inch piece of pre-gathered, 2-inch-wide lace
>
>   25-inch piece of 18-gauge jewelry wire
>
>   10- or 12-inch wood dowel
>
>   Red craft paint
>
>   Paintbrush
>
>   Bag of pink, white, and red foam hearts
>
>   Glue gun
>
>   Bunch of pink, white, and red satin ribbon roses (the ½-inch size)
>
>   Thin red satin ribbon
>
>   A Victorian-style Valentine's wreath

1. Thread the lace onto the wire, in and out of each hole at the inside edge of the lace. If you don't have gathered lace, you can use straight lace and gather it in place along the wire. Make sure the lace lies flat when placed on a hard surface. Bend the ends of the wire together and form a loop out of one of them for hanging purposes. Keeping the loop in the center, bend the wire into a heart shape.

2. Paint the dowel with red craft paint and allow it to dry. Thread the dowel through the heart from side to side on an angle. The dowel will keep the wire and lace heart from bending out of shape. Glue a foam heart on each end of the dowel, keeping the pointed side out for the tip of the arrow and the curved side out for the end of the arrow.

You can change the look of the lace heart wreath by using dried roses and baby's breath in the center as decorations instead of hearts and satin roses. You also might want to try making a grapevine heart-shape wreath by wiring eucalyptus branches and dried or satin flowers around the wreath and topping it off with a satin bow.

Guess What?

Laces and ribbons probably became a symbol of love stemming from the days of knighthood. Knights would go into battle carrying a piece of ribbon or lace given to them by their beloved ladies.

3. Glue pink, red, and white foam hearts around the middle of the heart on top of the wire base. Glue a contrasting color of satin rose on top of each heart. The hearts should be big enough to show beneath the roses (approximately one inch).

4. Make a small bow out of the satin ribbon and glue it to the top of the heart.

You might want to try making painted doodle bugs with your kids using tempera paints and copy or construction paper. First, fold the paper in half. Open up the paper and help your child paint his or her name with heavy paint on the top half of the paper along the fold line. Fold the paper in half again to form a creature made out of the child's name. Let your kids paint the bug and add features such as wings, stripes, eyes, antennae, and so on. See who can come up with the most creative names for their bugs.

You might want to invest in opaque paint markers to simplify the process of painting on craft projects. The markers are easy to use and work well on glass, ceramics, paper, wood, and just about any surface except fabric. To use the markers, shake well and press the tip on the surface until the paint starts to flow (in approximately 10 to 60 seconds). Repeat this step as needed during use. Keep the markers capped when not in use.

Shrinkable Shapes

Here's a new product you'll want to shrink! You can help your kids make funky jewelry, magnets, key chains, and more with shrinkable plastic. Just get them started and let their imaginations take over to create their own unique designs.

Sample shrink shapes to copy.

(Melissa LeBon)

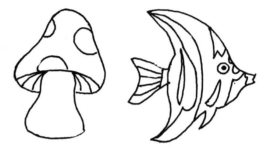

Level: Easy

Time involved: One to two hours

Materials:

Shrinkable plastic (You can find this in craft stores.)

Opaque paint markers or acrylic paints (Use only permanent markers or paints, not watercolors.)

Paintbrushes

Transfer or carbon paper and pen (optional)

Hole punch for jewelry (optional)

Brown paper bag

Baking sheet

Oven or toaster oven

Jewelry and barrette forms (optional)

Magnet sheet (optional)

Key-chain forms (optional)

Glue gun

1. Paint or draw on the rough side of the shrinkable plastic and allow it to dry. You could use your imagination or trace the sample illustrated designs onto the plastic using transfer or carbon paper. Just trace the sample design onto a piece of copy paper or tracing paper. Place the transfer or carbon paper over the rough side of the plastic. Lay the copy paper on top of this and trace the design again using a pen. The design will appear on the plastic. Cut the designs out of the shrinkable plastic. Punch any holes you need in the designs with a hole punch before baking it. (The hole will shrink to about half the size.)

2. Place the designs on a piece of brown paper and then on a cookie sheet with the decorated side up. Bake in an oven at 325°F for one to three minutes. After the pieces lie flat, bake for 30 seconds more. Remove the designs from the oven and allow them to cool.

3. Glue the designs onto jewelry forms, magnets, key chains, and so on.

Flocked Box

Create a Valentine's Day work of art with your kids by making this professional-looking flocked box to hold their jewelry or trinkets.

Steps to making a flocked heart box.

(Melissa LeBon)

Level: Moderately easy

Time involved: One to two hours, plus overnight to dry

Materials:

Newspaper or plastic

Heart-shape cardboard box

White craft paint

Paintbrush

Shallow cardboard box lined with waxed paper

Valentine's Day stencils of choice

Masking tape

Spouncer (stencil brush)

Red soft flock kit (Plaid makes this product, which contains adhesive and fibers and can be found in craft stores.)

1. Cover your work area with newspapers or plastic. Paint the outside of the heart-shape box and lid with white craft paint and allow it to dry.

2. Place the heart-shape box on the shallow box lined with waxed paper. Position the stencils in the middle of the lid of the heart-shape box and tape them in place. Load a damp spouncer (stencil brush) with a liberal amount of adhesive. Holding it vertically, spounce (dab) the adhesive through the stencil.

3. Immediately remove the stencil and apply the fibers. Hold the fiber bottle three to four inches from the stencil and squeeze short bouts of fibers onto the stencil with a continuous flow. Apply a liberal layer of fibers. Do not shake or tap the box; allow it to dry at least an hour before moving it. If desired, you can stencil the sides of the box with different stencils in the same manner.

4. Allow the box to cure overnight before using it. You might want to flock the inside of the box by painting it with red craft paint first and allowing it to dry. Then, paint a layer of the adhesive onto the inside of the box. Apply the fibers to the adhesive as described in step 2 and allow this to dry.

Plain and Simple

Soft flock is a trademarked product that creates a velvety effect on projects. The kit, made by Plaid, contains a bottle of adhesive and a bottle of tiny fibers. You can use your own stencils and stencil brush (spouncer) to brush a pattern of adhesive onto your project. Then, use the bottle of fibers and spray them onto the adhesive by squeezing the bottle and releasing it, creating short blasts of fiber. Place the project on a box lined with waxed paper to collect (and reuse) any excess fibers. Do not move the project until it has dried at least an hour. Be careful using this product if you are allergic to fibers (a mask and protective eyewear are recommended).

Kitchen Fun

Ever notice how the kitchen is the heart of the home? Families naturally congregate in the kitchen for everything including meals, homework, after-school snacks, family discussions, and school projects. Make the most of this family enclave by cooking up some kitchen fun.

Basket of Love

Puffy dough is a versatile craft medium. You can mold it into various shapes or roll it out and cut it into shapes with cookie cutters. The shapes will harden when baked to form permanent objects that can be painted. You might want to try your hand at making this unique basket out of cut-out hearts.

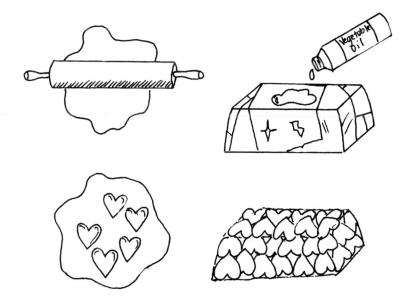

Creating a puffy dough basket.

(Melissa LeBon)

Level: Moderately difficult

Time involved: Three to four hours, plus overnight to dry

Ingredients:

    2 cups flour

    1 cup salt

1 cup water

Vegetable oil

Equipment:

Mixing bowl

Rolling pin

Heart-shape cookie cutter (approximately 2 inches wide)

Loaf pan

Tinfoil

Cookie sheet

Cooling rack

Varnish

Paintbrush

1. Mix the flour, salt, and water in a mixing bowl. Knead the ingredients with your hands until they are well blended. If the mixture is too runny, add more flour; if it's too stiff, add more water. Roll the dough onto a lightly floured surface to about ¼ inch and cut out the hearts with the cookie cutter.

2. Turn the loaf pan upside down and line the bottom and sides with tinfoil. Grease the tinfoil with a layer of vegetable oil. Start on the bottom of the pan and layer the cut-out hearts covering the entire surface and overlapping the sides and bottoms of the hearts. Press the dough together to cover any open spaces between the hearts. Continue this process on all sides of the pan until the entire bottom of the pan is covered with dough hearts. Pinch the hearts together on the edges of the pan to form a continuous basket form.

3. Place the pan on a cookie sheet and bake in a 350°F oven for 15 to 20 minutes or until the dough begins to brown on the edges. The dough should be firm to the touch. Remove the basket from the oven and carefully pry the dough off the loaf pan. Remove any tinfoil that sticks to the basket. Allow it to cool on a cooling rack.

Guess What?

In the Middle Ages, men picked names from a bowl to see who would be their Valentines. The men would wear the names on their sleeves for a week. Thus the saying "wearing your heart on your sleeve" originated.

4. Coat the basket with a thin layer of varnish inside and out and allow it to dry. Apply a second thin layer and allow this to dry overnight.

5. Line the basket with pink plastic wrap before filling it with cookies or other food products.

Creative Concoctions

You'll need some homemade cookies to put in your dough basket. Make these delicious butter cookies and let the kids help decorate them with gel icings.

Level: Moderately easy

Time involved: Two to three hours

Ingredients:

Basic Butter Cookie recipe:

> 4 sticks butter (Do not substitute margarine.)
>
> 2 cups sugar
>
> 1 egg, beaten
>
> 1 tsp. vanilla
>
> 4 cups flour
>
> Powdered sugar
>
> Gel icing

Equipment:

> Electric mixer
>
> Rolling pin
>
> Cookie cutters
>
> Cookie sheet
>
> Cooling racks

1. Cream the butter and sugar in an electric mixer until well blended. Add the beaten egg and vanilla and mix together. Add the flour gradually until you have a smooth, stiff dough mixture.

2. Refrigerate the dough for one hour before using. Roll the dough out ¼-inch thick onto a surface dusted with powdered sugar. Dip the cookie cutters in powdered sugar and cut shapes out of the rolled dough. Place the shapes on a cookie sheet and bake in a 350°F oven for approximately 10 minutes. The edges of the cookies will be golden brown when fully cooked.

3. Remove the cookies from the oven and cool them on cooling racks. Decorate the cookies with gel frostings.

Stolen Hearts

A decorative box of homemade chocolate hearts will stave off the chocolate cravings of your favorite Valentines. Make these for your friends and family or keep some hidden for those moments when nothing will do except a bite of chocolate.

Forming hearts and flowers on your chocolate candies.

(Melissa LeBon)

Level: Easy

Time involved: Two to three hours

Ingredients:

1-lb. bag brown melting chocolate (This can be found in blocks or discs in supermarkets or craft stores.)

1-lb. bag white melting chocolate

½ lb. pink melting chocolate

½ lb. green melting chocolate

Equipment:

Double boiler (or two pans that fit inside each other)

Heart-shape candy molds

Two sandwich bags

Scissors

1. Place about one inch of water in the bottom of the double boiler and bring it to a boil over medium-high heat. Put the brown chocolate in the top pan of the double boiler and place it on top of the bottom pan.

2. Lower the heat to medium low and cook the chocolate until melted. Once the chocolate begins to bubble, it's ready to pour. Don't overcook the chocolate or it will scorch and taste burnt.

3. Pour the chocolate into the heart molds. Allow these to harden, and then place them in the refrigerator for two hours before removing the chocolate from the molds. Carefully push the chocolate from the molds, applying pressure to the back of them.

4. Repeat steps 1 through 3 using the white chocolate.

5. Melt the pink chocolate and place it in a sandwich bag. Squeeze the chocolate to one corner and cut a small hole in this corner. Squeeze the pink chocolate into a flower or heart shape on top of each of the chocolate hearts and allow it to harden.

6. Melt the green chocolate and place it in a sandwich bag with a small hole cut in one corner. Squeeze the green chocolate onto the hearts with flowers to form leaves. You might want to make a green arrow on the pink heart shapes.

7. Allow the candies to harden in the refrigerator overnight before packing them into a container.

You might want to buy and decorate a candy box for your chocolate hearts. If you check out the box section of a craft store, you'll find white glossy boxes that you can decorate with stencils, paint, rub-on transfers, and so on. I found a box that resembles a cigar box that would be the perfect size for storing candies. You can also use a plastic box and decorate it with painted wooden shapes, foam shapes, or strips of fabric and specialty buttons arranged in a pattern on the lid.

Chapter

12

Easter Excitement

By the time Easter rolls around each year, most of us are ready to shed our coats and race outdoors to celebrate this spring event. A break in the weather and the renewal that occurs in nature is the perfect setting for an Easter celebration that thoughtfully considers the sacrifice Jesus made for us on the cross and the awesome wonder of the Resurrection. The arrival of spring heralds the hope of rebirth and new life.

For Christians, Easter Sunday commemorates the Resurrection of our Savior, Jesus Christ. Many Christian denominations begin with the 40-day observance of Lent, which begins on Ash Wednesday and concludes at Midnight on Holy Saturday. Easter is a movable feast and is celebrated on a Sunday between March 22 and April 25. Easter is definitely a holiday for celebrating family, and The Good News of Easter was meant to be shared with others. As you think about old and new family traditions for Easter, think about how those traditions can be used to introduce others to the excitement of the season.

Easter Enjoyment

Even though many of the symbols of Easter may have originated in the pre-Christian spring festivals, as Christians we can reclaim many of these (after all, God created eggs and bunnies) as symbols of the new life Jesus' death and Resurrection provide to us.

Easter time is the perfect holiday to spend spring break with the kids working together on special crafts. You can indulge the kid in you by making these Easter symbols to place around your home.

Guess What?

The Christian celebration of Easter embodies a number of converging traditions with emphasis on the relationship of Easter to the Jewish festival of Passover, commemorating the flight and freedom of the Israelites from slavery in Egypt. Because many of the early Christians were of Jewish origin and brought up in the Hebrew tradition, many in the early church regarded Easter as a new feature of the Passover festival in honor of the advent of the Messiah as foretold by the prophets.

Little Lambies

It was the blood of a lamb that caused the angel of death to pass over the homes of the Israelites in Egypt, sparing their first born. It is the death and Resurrection of Jesus, the Lamb that was slain for our sins, that we celebrate at Easter. These little lambies will look adorable on your mantel or bookshelf, but they are also a fun craft for the kids to make. You can even hang a name tag around each neck and use them for place markers at your Easter dinner table.

Make an entire flock of these fluffy lambs.

Level: Moderately easy

Time involved: One to two hours

Materials:

> $2\frac{1}{2}$-inch white pom-poms
>
> $1\frac{1}{2}$-inch white pom-poms
>
> $\frac{1}{2}$-inch white pom-poms
>
> $\frac{1}{4}$-inch black pom-poms
>
> Black felt scraps for ears
>
> Small black beads for eyes
>
> Scissors
>
> Craft glue or hot glue gun
>
> Pink or black fabric paint
>
> $\frac{1}{4}$-inch ribbon
>
> 9mm jingle bells

1. Glue $1\frac{1}{2}$-inch pom-pom (head) to $2\frac{1}{2}$-inch white pom-pom (body) with craft glue or hot glue gun. (*Caution:* Children should be supervised at all times if a glue gun is being used.)
2. Cut out small oval-shape ears from scraps of black felt and glue to side of head.
3. Use scissors to trim muzzle on head. Imagine a line across the face from ear to ear—that is where you will start to trim. Trim down from the line to shape a muzzle for your lamb.
4. Glue small beads on trimmed head for eyes. Add $\frac{1}{2}$-inch white pompom for tail and glue four black $\frac{1}{4}$-inch pompoms on the underside of the body for legs.
5. Use fabric paint to make mouth.
6. Thread ribbon through bell and tie around lamb's neck.

Once you get the hang of making these fuzzy little fluff balls, you will have a whole flock in no time.

That's the Spirit

"For you know that God paid a ransom to save you from the empty life you inherited from your ancestors. And the ransom he paid was not mere gold or silver. He paid for you with the precious life-blood of Christ, the sinless, spotless Lamb of God ... Through Christ you have come to trust in God. And because God raised Christ from the dead and gave him great glory, your faith and hope can be placed confidently in God." (1 Peter 1:18–19, 21) This is the Good News of Easter.

Old-Tyme Easter Basket

Putting out an Easter basket is a traditional Easter activity that kids love. You and your kids can make special baskets that look like they were handed down from their grandparents. Baskets are relatively inexpensive and can be found in all shapes and sizes. Be sure to pick one that has smooth wooden surfaces that can be painted and stenciled. Why not make an extra, add dried flowers, and give it to a friend or neighbor?

A unique Easter basket with an antique look.

Level: Moderately easy

Time involved: Two to three hours

Materials:

> Basket
>
> Fine-grain sandpaper
>
> Dry sponge
>
> Craft paints in colors and white
>
> Foam plate
>
> Paintbrushes
>
> Disposable cup
>
> Stencils
>
> Masking tape
>
> Stencil paint
>
> Stencil brush
>
> Permanent black marker
>
> Crepe paper and *crimper* (optional)
>
> Dried flowers (optional)

1. Lightly sand the basket to rough up a surface for the paint. Brush off any particles with a dry sponge.

2. Paint the entire basket inside and out with craft paint in any color you choose. Allow the basket to dry.

3. Mix about ⅓ cup white craft paint in a disposable cup with 6 tablespoons water. Brush the paint mixture on top of the color paint. The color paint should show through the white coating. If the white paint is too thick, add a little water; if too thin, add more white paint.

4. Using a wet sponge, rub some of the white paint off in places to allow more of the color to show through. Allow the white coat to dry.

Plain and Simple

def·i·ni·tion

A **crimper** is a tool that will cut different shapes out of paper products such as tissue paper, crepe paper, or construction paper. You can use these shreds of paper in baskets or gift bags for filler. If you own a paper shredder, you also might want to consider using it to make this filler.

5. Tape the stencils around the top rim of the basket (or on the handle if thick enough) and fill in the stencils with the appropriate color of stencil paint. You might want to make bunnies, Easter eggs, and flowers in a pattern. Allow the stencils to dry.

6. Using the black permanent marker, personalize each basket, adding the date so your child will have a keepsake for years to come.

7. If desired, fill basket with crepe paper. You can use a paper crimper to make basket filler out of matching colors of crepe paper. Your kids now have a personalized basket that you can fill with Easter goodies. Or arrange an assortment of dried flowers in the basket and share with a friend or neighbor.

Cartin' Around Easter Goodies

You can cart around the Easter goodies in this colorful handmade wheelbarrow. Make these cute carts as decorations or fill them with Easter candies to give as gifts for your family or friends.

A quaint container for Easter goodies.

Level: Easy

Time involved: One to two hours

Materials:

> 54 wooden craft sticks
>
> Glue gun
>
> Wooden wheel
>
> White crackle-finish base coat
>
> Green crackle-finish spray paint
>
> Pastel-colored craft paints
>
> Foam plate
>
> Paintbrushes
>
> Clear acrylic finish spray
>
> Paper grass

1. Lay out 11 sticks in a row and glue 11 more sticks on top of and perpendicular to these. Glue four sticks around the perimeter of the top row of sticks (see illustration). Glue sticks on top of these sticks in the same manner to form a box that is four sticks high. (All the sticks are glued down flat, not on their sides.)

2. Build one end wall and two side walls three sticks higher, and slope the sides to the end wall that is four sticks high (see illustration).

3. Glue three sticks together as shown to form a handle. Repeat this process to form the second handle. Glue the ends of the handles onto the wooden wheel. Glue the handles in place on the bottom of the cart as shown. Cut a Popsicle stick into two two-inch pieces, and glue these onto the bottom of the cart to form a stand.

4. Spray the base coat of the crackle paint onto the finished cart. Allow this to dry and then spray the top coat on the cart. Allow this to dry.

Family Ties

Making crafts together can be only the beginning of your family fun. Sharing the crafts with others can multiply your joy. Why not give one of your Easter crafts to a neighbor or take one to a shut-in from your church?

5. You might want to add some colored-paper grass to the cart before adding chocolate eggs and jelly beans into the grass.

You can turn this cute Easter cart into an Autumn project by adding small wooden pumpkins and colored leaves to it instead of Easter goodies. A red cart with miniature Christmas ornaments and holly glued inside would also make a unique Christmas tree ornament.

Steps to assembling an Easter cart.

(Melissa LeBon)

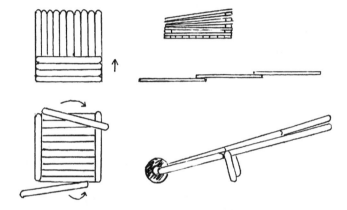

Lacy Eggs

Gather your family together to help you make these beautiful Easter eggs that you can use year after year. You might want to spray-paint an egg carton with an Easter color to keep them safe in between use.

Level: Moderately easy

Time involved: Two to three hours, including drying time

Materials:

Dozen eggs

Bowl

Straight pin

Nail

Toothpick

Dark green, maroon, navy, and yellow glossy craft paints

Paintbrushes

Foam tray

Assorted pieces of lace (Use the type of lace that has distinct designs that can be cut out.)

Scissors

Craft glue

Clear acrylic finish spray

Making a lacy Easter egg.

(Melissa LeBon)

Guess What?

The egg has long been a symbol of Easter, dating back to the custom of giving colored, hard-boiled eggs or chocolate eggs as gifts during pagan festivals. Christians view eggs as a symbol of the new life Christ's Resurrection provides to us. Before the era of Christianity, Egyptians dyed Easter eggs in spring colors to symbolize renewed life.

1. Hold an egg over a bowl. Using a straight pin, poke a hole in both ends of the egg. Use the nail to enlarge the hole by slightly twisting it into the started holes. Make the hole about ¼-inch wide. Stir the egg inside with a toothpick, and shake the egg to remove the mixture. Rinse the egg inside and out and allow to dry.

2. Paint the egg with a high-gloss craft paint of your choice and allow to dry.

3. Cut out designs from the lace pieces. Glue these in a pattern on the egg. Be sure to cover both holes with a piece of cut-out lace. Allow to dry.

4. Spray the egg with clear acrylic finish spray and allow to dry.

5. Repeat these steps using different colors and lace patterns until all the eggs are decorated.

You might want to try substituting paper doilies for the lace used in making lacey eggs. You can also make these eggs with glued-on sequins or acrylic jewels. Display the finished products by hanging them on a tree branch that is sprayed white and placed in a pot of dirt covered with Spanish moss. To hang an egg, insert a small piece of a toothpick with embroidery thread tied around the middle of it into the hole before covering it. Pull up on the thread until the toothpick is sideways against the inside of the hole and holds the thread in place.

Egg-Ceptional Eggs

There are lots of techniques and natural dyes for making unique, personalized, colored Easter eggs. If you're ready for a change of pace, try some of these eggs to dye for.

- **Using natural dyes.** The technique for dyeing eggs with natural dyes is to add the ingredients to ¾ cup boiling water and then add ½ teaspoon vinegar. Always wash the eggs first with soapy water to remove any oily coating. Simmer the egg for about 20 minutes in the dye. Natural dyes include instant coffee, spinach, orange peels, lemon peels, blueberries, cranberries, red beets, and ground turmeric. If you want your eggs a darker color, refrigerate them in the dye overnight.

- **Making designs.** Cover the egg with rubber bands, crayon markings, or pieces of masking tape before dyeing them. The area that is covered will not take the dye and will form a design on the egg. Re-dip the eggs in another color if desired.

- **Using tissue or crepe paper dye.** Soak tissue or crepe paper in hot water. Place pieces of the paper on the egg for a few minutes and remove them. The dye from the paper will remain on the egg.

- **Creating sponge effects.** Use food coloring and small sponges to create a splattered effect on your eggs. Be sure to wear gloves for this project.

- **Making an egg farm.** Use construction paper, feathers, pom-poms, pipe cleaners, and rub-on faces to make farm animals out of dyed eggs. Form a strip of paper into a circle that fits snugly around the bottom of the egg. Make a face on the egg using rub-on transfer faces that can be found in a craft store. Add feathers, construction paper features, pipe cleaners, and pom-poms as desired.

> **Guess What?**
>
> You might want to save the shells from broken Easter eggs to make mosaics. Draw the outline of a cross or a floral arrangement on a piece of poster board. Crack the eggshells into small pieces and lay them on top of a thick layer of glue, filling in the picture or design. Allow the glue to dry several hours before moving the picture.

Easter Egg Hunt

An Easter Egg Hunt is a great activity that can involve everyone in the family when planned to include others. Adults and older children can help stuff plastic eggs with goodies and find good hiding places for them—indoors or out depending on your springtime climate. Here are some tips for a successful hunt:

- Gather supplies from discount and thrift stores: Inexpensive plastic eggs and baskets are usually readily available in the weeks before Easter. Try to provide each child who will be attending your hunt with his or her own basket or a pretty gift bag.

- Make stuffing the eggs a family affair. On family activity night a week or so before Easter, get everyone in the family involved in stuffing the eggs. You can use wrapped candy, stickers, small toys, money, whatever fits your budget and the ages of the children. Count the eggs so you know how many there are to find. To keep the hunt fair, have enough eggs so everyone will get the same amount.

- The day of the hunt, let adults or teens not participating in the hunt hide the eggs while the children are distracted by finishing up brunch or dinner or playing a game. Some eggs should be easy to find, others more difficult to accommodate the various ages of the children.

- Before the hunt begins, give each child a basket, bag, or other container to hold his or her eggs. Tell all the children how many eggs they can collect before they must stop hunting. Once they have their limit, they can still look but they cannot pick up any more. Have older children help younger ones if the little ones start to get frustrated.

You can avoid any hassle of kids of different ages competing for eggs in the hunt by writing their names on the eggs and having them look for their eggs only. Instruct the participants to re-hide any eggs they find that don't have their name on them.

If the hunt is for your family only, Mom and Dad might replace candy and toys with coupons for special treasures like a date alone with Dad or one chore-free day.

Jesus Is Risen!

Tell your kids the story of the Resurrection of Jesus Christ, and then make these window decorations with them to celebrate this victory over death.

Level: Moderately easy

Time involved: One to two hours and overnight to dry

Materials:

Plain and Simple

def·i·ni·tion

Styrene blanks are plastic sheets that are placed over a design and traced with paint, peel, and stick paints. These can be found in a craft store.

Resurrection pattern

Copy paper

Pen

Styrene blanks

Assorted colors of paint, peel, and stick-on transparent paint including black leading paint

A sample design for a risen-Lord window decoration.

(Melissa LeBon)

1. Trace the sample Resurrection pattern onto copy paper and place it under the styrene blank. Trace the pattern with leading paint onto the styrene blank and allow this to dry for one to two hours.

2. To fill in the design, squeeze the paint directly from the bottle, moving the bottle side to side and filling in the area to the same level as the leading. Allow this to dry for 24 hours or longer in humid climates.

3. Gently peel off the design from the styrene blank and stick it on a window or smooth surface.

You can make other Easter suncatchers using paint, peel, and stick-on transparent paint. These paints come in easy-to-use squeeze bottles. You might want to download some Easter designs from the Internet or use an Easter coloring book for ideas. Or you can always let your imagination take over and create your own designs.

Family Ties

Use a Bible storybook to share the Resurrection story with younger children. Or read the account from the Bible (consider using the New Living Translation). You might want to use the following schedule of daily readings for the week leading up to the Resurrection story on Easter Sunday:

Wednesday:	Mark 14:53–65
Thursday:	Luke 23:13–25
Friday:	Mark 15:24–37
Saturday:	Mark 15:37–47
Easter Sunday:	Matthew 28:1–9

Easter Edibles

Don't let this Easter season pass you by without making some special treats for your friends and family. Get everyone involved in the process and spend some rewarding hours together, bonding in the kitchen.

Miracle Rolls

These "ordinary" dinner rolls hold a surprise for your children and guests. Serve with an egg casserole and fruit for Easter breakfast or with your favorite Easter dinner dishes. When the rolls are baked, the marshmallow melts, leaving an "empty" space inside—creating a great object lesson for the true message of Easter, the empty tomb.

Level: Easy

Time involved: Under 30 minutes

Ingredients:

> 1 can refrigerated dinner rolls (8 rolls)
>
> 1 package large marshmallows
>
> Butter
>
> Jam or fruit spread

1. Pop open can of rolls, separate and flatten slightly.
2. Place one marshmallow in the center of each roll and fold the dough around the marshmallow.
3. Be sure to pinch and seal the dough tightly around the marshmallow; otherwise the marshmallow will leak out while baking.
4. Place rolls with seam down on a lightly greased cookie sheet. Brush tops with melted butter and bake at 375°F for 8 minutes.
5. Serve with jam or fruit spread.

Excellent Eggs

Easter wouldn't be Easter without the taste of homemade Easter eggs. These are candies that can't be topped. Lisa Gray of Pottsville, Pennsylvania, melts her chocolate in a microwave oven when making these candies to simplify the process.

Level: Moderately easy

Time involved: One to two hours

Ingredients:

Butter Cream Egg recipe:

> 1 stick (½ cup) butter
>
> 1 (8-oz.) pkg. cream cheese

2 lbs. powdered sugar

½ tsp. vanilla extract

Peanut Butter Egg recipe:

12 oz. peanut butter

4 oz. cream cheese

1-lb. box powdered sugar

1 tsp. vanilla extract

¼ tsp. salt

Coconut Cream Egg recipe:

½ stick (¼ cup) butter

8 oz. cream cheese

2 lbs. powdered sugar

1 tsp. vanilla extract

½ cup flake coconut

To coat the eggs:

1 lb. melting chocolate

½ tsp. vegetable oil

Equipment:

Mixer or food processor

Cookie sheets

Waxed paper

Microwave-safe bowl

Colander with holes (not slits) in the bottom

Wooden skewers

1. Using an electric mixer or food processor, mix the butter or peanut butter and cream cheese until blended. Add the remaining ingredients for the type of egg you're making, and blend approximately three minutes or until thoroughly mixed.

2. Refrigerate the mixture overnight. Using your hands, shape pieces of the mixture into small eggs. Place the eggs on a cookie sheet covered with waxed paper. Refrigerate for several hours until hardened.

3. After the eggs have hardened, place the chocolate pieces in a microwave-safe bowl. Add ½ teaspoon vegetable oil to the chocolate. Cook on medium heat for one minute. Remove the bowl from the microwave and stir. Return the bowl to the microwave oven and cook another minute or until the chocolate is thoroughly melted.

4. Turn the colander upside down on a piece of waxed paper. Remove the eggs from the refrigerator and place one on a wooden skewer. Dip the egg into the chocolate mixture until it is thoroughly coated. Stick the end of the skewer into one of the holes of the colander until it hardens (about two minutes). Once it hardens, remove the egg from the stick and return it to the cookie sheet. You can reuse the skewers for the rest of the eggs. Repeat this step until all the eggs are coated. If your chocolate begins to re-harden, you could cook it in the microwave oven again for a few seconds until it is melted. Place the coated eggs in the refrigerator for a couple hours until hardened. Store the eggs in the refrigerator in a plastic container between layers of waxed paper until you're ready to eat them.

Chapter 13

Parent Perfect

Mother's Day and Father's Day have been officially celebrated in the United States since the early 1900s. In 1872, Julia Ward Howe (author of the "Battle Hymn of the Republic") suggested that a special day be set aside for Mother's Day in America. Unfortunately, no one took her seriously. Anna Jarvis of West Virginia is considered to be the true founder of Mother's Day in America—she spent considerable time and energy campaigning for an official Mother's Day celebration. By 1909, almost every state had a planned Mother's Day holiday. In 1914, President Woodrow Wilson made Mother's Day an official celebration in the United States to be held on the second Sunday in May.

The Mother's Day celebration may have spurred the creation of a special day set aside for fathers. Sonora Smart Dodd of Spokane, Washington, was listening to a Mother's Day Sermon at her church in 1909. Her mother had died in childbirth, and her father was the sole parent taking care of 6 children for 21 years. Sonora campaigned to have an official day established to recognize fathers. It was decided to create Father's Day to be celebrated on June 5, her father's birthday. However, time constraints moved the first celebration to June 18. In 1972, the U.S. Congress officially recognized the celebration of Father's Day to be held on the third Sunday of June.

Whether you have a mother, father, grandparent, aunt, or uncle to remember, you can individualize their gifts by creating them with your own two hands. Get the kids involved in these activities to make the experience even more meaningful.

Marvelous Mothers

Lots of mothers are present in our lives. You may have a grandmother, a mother, a daughter or friend who's a mother, or an aunt who's like a mother to you. Whatever the case, you can't go wrong with these special crafts that do double duty as gifts on this special occasion.

Guess What?

The celebration of Mother's Day can be traced to ancient mythology. The Greeks and Romans had powerful goddesses whom they believed to be the mothers of all gods. Celebrations were held to honor these special women. The eventual rise of Christianity brought about the concept of holding a celebration to honor the "Mother Church." On the fourth Sunday in Lent, people brought gifts to the churches where they were baptized. In the 1600s, England instituted a special day of honor for mothers called "Mothering Day," which also occurred on the fourth Sunday in Lent.

Pretty Posy Pens

Moms always enjoy getting flowers. So imagine Mom's delight when she discovers that this bouquet is beautiful and functional. Personalize this craft by choosing colors and flowers that match your mother's taste. She'll be happy to set this lovely pen holder by any phone in her home—kitchen, bedroom, or den.

That's the Spirit

"Honor your father and mother." This is the first of the Ten Commandments that ends with a promise. And this is the promise: "If you honor your father and mother, you will live a long life, full of blessing." (Ephesians 6:2–3) Perhaps part of the blessing we receive in honoring our parents is having children who imitate our attitudes and actions and honor us.

Level: Moderately easy

Time involved: One to two hours

Materials:

Vase or other flower container

6 to 12 ballpoint pens (black, blue, or a mixture)

Tape

Floral tape

Silk flowers (Sometimes these are cheaper in a bunch, but make sure there are enough separate blossoms for your bouquet.)

Ribbon or raffia for bows

Wire cutters

Marbles

1. Use wire cutters to trim each flower stem to within three to four inches from blossom.

2. Tape blossom to top of stem. Using the floral tape, wrap from the top of the pen down, securing the flower stem to the pen. Repeat until you have enough pen blossoms to make a nice bouquet.

3. Tie ribbon or raffia bow around container and add marbles. Place pen posies point down into the container and arrange.

Family Ties

> The most important thing a father can do for his children is to love their mother.
> —Theodore Hesburgh

Okay, Dad! You can do crafts, too! Why not send Mom out for the afternoon and help your kids make one of these crafts for her for Mother's Day? They're easy and inexpensive, you'll have fun spending time with your kids, and you will be teaching them an important love lesson.

Mosaic Stepping-Stone

Your mom will think of you every time she steps into her garden on this lovely stepping-stone. If desired, you can add a personal touch to this stone by making a heart out of the decorative pieces and spelling out "Mom."

Stepping into the garden with Mom.

Level: Moderately difficult

Time involved: Three to four hours, plus two days to dry

Materials:

> Box of stepping-stone cement mix (You can find this in craft stores prepackaged in the size you'll need for the mold.)
>
> Water
>
> Bucket
>
> Garden digging tool or trowel to mix the cement
>
> Stepping-stone mold
>
> Decorative glass chips or marbles
>
> Popsicle stick (optional)
>
> Sponge
>
> Mosaic sealant
>
> Paintbrush

1. Mix the cement and water in a bucket according to the manufacturer's directions. Use the trowel or digging tool to turn the cement over and work in the powder.

2. Pour the cement into the stepping-stone mold and level off the top using the trowel or digging tool.

3. Place the decorative glass or marbles on top of the cement in a planned or random pattern. If desired, form a heart and the words "Best Mom" on top of the cement. You could also use the Popsicle stick to write a name or saying (such as "Mom's Garden") in the cement.

4. Be sure to work quickly and have your design completed before the cement begins to set. (You have approximately one hour to complete your design.) Wipe the design lightly with a wet sponge to remove any excess cement. Once you've completed your stone, do not move the mold until it has completely set (overnight), or you'll develop cracks in the stone.

5. Once the stone is completely hardened, you can remove it from the mold by applying pressure to the back of the mold. Paint the stone with *mosaic sealant* and allow it to dry overnight.

def·i·ni·tion

Plain and Simple

Mosaic sealant comes in a small can, and you can find it in craft stores in the mosaic section. This sealant works well on cement and glass, but I wouldn't advise using it on plaster molds (clear acrylic finish spray works better on plaster). You can paint the sealant onto the project, and you should allow it to dry overnight. You'll need paint remover to clean your brush afterward.

Handy Candy Container

Mom will love this cute candy dish filled with her favorite wrapped sweets. You could also make a smaller version of this pot and fill it with potpourri or a scented candle.

Sweets for a sweet mom.

Level: Moderately easy

Time involved: Three to four hours, including drying time

Materials:

   Newspaper or plastic

   4-inch clay pot

   2 (4-inch) clay saucers

   Antique-white craft paint

Paintbrush

Round wooden knob

Red, blue, and brown craft paints

Glue gun

Clear acrylic finish spray

Piece of felt for the bottom

Scissors

Tacky glue

1. Place newspapers or plastic on your work area to protect it. Paint the clay pot and the saucers inside and out with the antique-white paint. Paint the wooden knob antique white. Allow these to dry.

2. Paint a blue spiral design on the wooden knob. Glue the knob to the bottom of the clay saucer to form a lid with a handle. Paint the word "Candy" on the rim of this lid. Paint a blue lollipop and red and white peppermint candy on the front of the candy dish. Paint a blue line on the bottom of the candy dish for an accent.

3. Glue the bottom of the second saucer onto the bottom of the pot.

4. Spray the pot with clear acrylic finish spray and allow it to dry. Cut a piece of felt the size of the bottom of the finished candy dish and glue it onto the bottom saucer using tacky glue.

Father's Day Favorites

Don't neglect the "fathers" in your life. Make them a special Father's Day gift to show them you appreciate all of their love and support over the years.

Gone Fishin'

If your father's into fishing, you might want to make him this personalized fishing tackle box. He'll think of you every time he reaches for a new hook.

Level: Moderately easy

Time involved: Two to three hours, including drying time

Materials:

Foam stamps with a nautical theme (fish, plants, shells, anchors, and so on)

Craft paints

Foam plate

Paintbrushes

White copy paper

Scissors

Decoupage finish

Plastic fishing tackle box (Choose one with a smooth surface.)

Sticker letters

Adding a personal touch to a practical gift.

(Melissa LeBon)

1. Paint one of the nautical stamps with colorful craft paints. Press the prepared stamp onto the copy paper. Repeat this process with other stamps and colors. Allow the stamps to dry.

2. Cut out the images, and brush the decoupage finish on the back of them. Place the stamps in a pattern around the tackle box and smooth them in place with your fingers. Allow this to dry completely.

3. Spell out your father's name and the words "Tackle Box" on the front of the box using the sticker letters.

4. Brush *decoupage finish* over the tackle box and allow it to dry. Repeat with a second coat.

def·i·ni·tion Plain and Simple

You can find **decoupage finish** in the decoupage section of craft stores. To use this medium, simply cut out your designs from paper or fabric. Brush a light coat of decoupage finish on the back of the cut-out design. Place this on your project and smooth it in place with your fingers. When this is completely dry, brush the decoupage finish over the entire project and repeat with a second coat.

Cook's Cover-Up

Does your father or husband flip the best burgers in town? Is his favorite meal something from the grill and a frosty mug of root beer? You might want to create a special apron for him for Father's Day that he'll be proud to wear at your next barbecue.

Making a design on a canvas apron.

(Melissa LeBon)

Level: Moderately easy

Time involved: Two to three hours, plus overnight to dry

Materials:

Canvas or denim apron (You can find these in craft or discount department stores.)

Iron and ironing board

Iron-on transfer with a food theme (optional)

Scissors (optional)

Pencil or crayon to draw a design (optional)

Straight pins

Piece of cardboard

Fabric paints in squeeze bottles

Paintbrushes (optional)

1. Wash and dry the apron without using fabric softener. Press it to remove any wrinkles.

2. If using a transfer, turn on the iron to a cotton setting. Cut out the transfer, leaving a 1-inch border. Pin the design to the apron, ink side down. Press with the iron for about 10 seconds. Don't move the iron or the design will blur. Lift one corner to see if it is transferred; if not, repeat the ironing process. Remove the transfer from the apron. Pin the apron to the piece of cardboard and fill in the areas with fabric paint in squeeze bottles.

3. If creating your own design, draw the outline on the apron with a pencil or crayon and color it in with the appropriate colors of fabric paint. You can also follow the design in the illustration. You might want to dilute the fabric paint with a little water and use a paintbrush to paint larger areas of the design.

4. If desired, leave room on the bib of the apron to write a saying such as "World's Greatest Cook" or "Chef (father or husband's name)."

5. Allow the apron to dry overnight. After 72 hours the apron can be washed when necessary by using warm water in a gentle cycle.

Guess What?

You can follow several techniques when using fabric paints in squeeze bottles. You can paint right from the bottle so that the applicator tip touches the surface of the fabric. Allow the paint to seep into the fabric by squeezing the bottle and dragging the tip along the design. You can also brush on fabric paint mixed with extender or water to fill in larger areas.

To add shading to a design, paint a darker color over a lighter color where the light would hit the object. Make dots or teardrops on your project by squeezing the bottle quickly, barely touching the fabric, and then lifting up the bottle. Make a dot and drag the bottle to the side to make a teardrop. Don't make a long continuous line when using fabric paints because it will tend to crack when the fabric moves.

Family Fun

The whole family can enjoy "messing around" together with these kid-approved crafts. Make something for Mom or Dad, or just spend some quality time together being creative.

Flutterflies

Celebrate the arrival of spring by helping your kids make this flying stained-glass butterfly. This would be a perfect decoration for Mom and Dad's garden or deck.

Making a stained-glass flutterfly.

(Melissa LeBon)

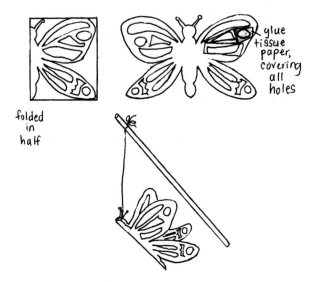

folded in half

glue tissue paper, covering all holes

Level: Easy

Time involved: One to two hours

Materials:

Construction paper

Pencil

Scissors

Tissue paper

White glue

Clear contact paper

Hole punch

String or yarn

Dowel

1. Fold a piece of construction paper in half. (Choose a bright color for your butterfly.) Draw an outline of a butterfly on the paper as shown. Be sure the body of the butterfly is in the fold. Cut out several holes in the wings with scissors for the stained-glass effect.

2. Cut out the shape and trace it onto another piece of construction paper. You should have two identical butterfly shapes.

3. Glue pieces of tissue paper onto one side of a butterfly cut-out, covering the holes. Glue the second butterfly on top of this. (The tissue paper should be sandwiched between the two construction-paper butterflies.)

4. Lay the butterfly onto the sticky side of a piece of clear contact paper. Place a second piece of clear contact paper on the other side so that both sides of the butterfly are covered. Trim around the outside of the butterfly. Make a hole in the top of the butterfly with a hole punch or sharp scissors to attach the string.

5. Bend the butterfly in half and attach it to a string. Attach the string to a wooden dowel.

If your kids enjoyed making a flutterfly, you can try making a bird using the same technique. You can also string the stained-glass creations from a wire hanger, creating a mobile for a kid's bedroom.

Foam Frames

You can make a magnetic picture frame for Mom or Dad using foam sheets. Either buy pre-cut foam frames with magnets attached (check out your local craft store), or design your own frame out of foam sheets.

Level: Easy

Time involved: One to two hours

Materials:

Two 5 × 5-inch purple foam sheets (or your choice of colors)

Pencil

Two different-size drinking glasses (to make circles)

Scissors

Magnet

Glue gun

Blue, green, red, and purple jewelry wire

Wire cutters

Bag of foam animals with a spring theme (chicks, ducks, and so on)

Photo

A pretty frame for a kid's photo.

1. Place the smaller glass in the middle of the foam sheet and trace around it to form a space for the photo. Draw the shape of a flower on the foam sheet, keeping the circle in the center. Cut the flower out of the foam sheet. Cut the circle out of the center of the flower. The flower with a circle cut out of it will form the picture frame.

2. Use a larger-based glass to draw another circle on the second piece of purple foam sheet. Cut out this circle to make a backing for your frame. Glue a magnet onto one side of the circle.

3. Form a heart and flower out of the jewelry wire and glue them each onto a side of the front of the frame.

4. Pick out three foam animals and glue them to the top and bottom of the frame. Cut a photo in a circular shape, using the smaller glass to make the circle. Glue this picture onto the purple circle on the side without the magnet.

5. Position the flower frame over the circle with the photo, and glue it together around the edges of the circle.

Family Ties

Grandmothers, mothers, or aunts would love a handcrafted gift from their favorite tykes. You might want to help your kids make a handprint frame for these special people. Just have the kids trace their handprints onto special textured paper (scrapbook paper works well) and cut them out. Glue the handprints around the perimeter of a cardboard frame and place a picture of the kids in the frame.

Crafty Kitchen Creations

There's nothing like the homemade taste of a special treat from your kitchen. These recipes are easy to make and create hours of family fun. They also make a great gift for Mother's or Father's Day!

Chocolate-Covered Delights

Chocolate-covered strawberries are a delicious and perfect treat for a special occasion. You can add variety to your creations by using dark and white chocolate to dip the berries.

When cooking chocolate in a double boiler, be sure to keep it at medium heat or lower. If the mixture begins to boil, turn it down. If the chocolate is boiled too long, it won't have the right consistency to cover the strawberries. It could also scorch and have a burnt taste. Don't leave the strawberries in the chocolate for more than a second or two, or they'll become soggy.

That's the Spirit

Kind words are like honey—sweet to the soul and healthy for the body.
—Proverbs 16:24

Of all the gifts you can give to honor your parents, kind words are the best. Why not write your dad or mom a note telling them just how much they mean to you? Kind words that are written keep giving day after day after day.

Level: Moderately easy

Time involved: One to two hours

Ingredients:

> Large dipping strawberries
>
> ½ lb. dark dipping chocolate
>
> ½ lb. white dipping chocolate

Equipment:

> Double boiler
>
> Cookie sheet
>
> Waxed paper

1. Wash the strawberries and allow them to dry. Do not remove the stems.
2. Place ½ inch water in the double boiler and bring it to a boil. Put the dark chocolate in the top boiler pan. Cook over medium heat until the chocolate is melted.
3. Meanwhile, lay some sheets of waxed paper on the cookie sheet.
4. Once the chocolate is melted, hold a strawberry by the stem and dip into the chocolate for a second. Don't cover the stem with chocolate. Remove the strawberry and place it stem side down on the prepared cookie sheet. Repeat this process with half the strawberries.
5. Repeat steps 2 through 4 using white chocolate in the pan. Store the strawberries in a plastic container until ready to use. Serve on a cut glass or china plate covered with a lace doily.

Add a poem, a handmade card, or a bottle of sparkling cider for a special treat.

Taffy

Round up the kids and get them involved in a taffy-pulling session to create this sweet concoction for Mom or Dad.

Level: Moderately easy

Time involved: One to two hours

Ingredients:

 2 cups sugar

 ⅔ cup light corn syrup

 ⅔ cup water

 ½ tsp. vanilla extract

 3 TB. butter or margarine

 Butter to grease cookie sheets

Equipment:

 Heavy saucepan

 Candy thermometer

 Cookie sheets

 Spatula

 Kitchen shears

1. Mix the sugar, corn syrup, and water in a heavy saucepan. Add the butter or margarine and insert a candy thermometer into the mixture. Heat, stirring constantly, over moderately high heat until the sugar dissolves. Cook uncovered without stirring to 270°F or until a drop placed in cold water forms firm, pliable strands.

2. Pour the mixture all at once onto a cookie sheet greased with butter. Do not scrape the pan. Cool one to two minutes, and then sprinkle with the vanilla. Using a buttered spatula, fold the edges in toward the center to distribute the heat evenly.

3. When the candy is cool enough to handle, pull and stretch it with buttered hands until it is light and no longer shiny. When it is too stiff to pull anymore, stretch the taffy into a rope about ½ inch in diameter, and with kitchen shears greased with butter, cut across the grain into 1-inch pieces. Separate the pieces and dry thoroughly, and then wrap and store them in an airtight container.

Making delicious taffy with the kids.

(Melissa LeBon)

Guess What?

The exact origin of the sweet confection known as taffy is not known. However, we do know that it was sold at Midwest country fairs and Atlantic City in the 1880s. It was Joseph Fralinger who first packaged taffy in boxes to sell on the boardwalk of the Jersey Shore. His long, skinny-shape candies are distinguished from those of another taffy legend, Enoch James. James' produces square bite-size taffy pieces known as a "kiss."

Chapter 14

Patriotic Pride

Official holidays mark the beginning, the middle, and the end of the summer season in the United States. The first of these holidays, Memorial Day, commemorates the memory of loved ones who have died and our soldiers who died in battle. The Fourth of July celebrates the birth of our nation, and Labor Day honors working Americans. These three holidays have a common thread—the reaffirmation of the patriotic pride that pervades the American spirit. We celebrate federal holidays by hanging the American flag and counting the many blessings that accompany living in a free nation. It's a great time to kick back at a summer barbecue or vacation spot and spend some welcome time off with family and friends.

If you have vacation time, you might want to check out the crafts in this chapter. Gather your loved ones together for a fun craft session and display your patriotic colors with pride.

Memorable Memorial Day

Memorial Day, celebrated the last Monday in May, is our time to remember that the freedoms we enjoy in this country are not free. It is a time to connect with the generations who have gone before us—talk about those in your family who have served both God and country. Make a "Frozen Flower" bouquet to share with someone who has lost a loved one this past year.

Frozen Flowers

The nice thing about a break in the weather that occurs around Memorial Day is the beginning of the growing season. You can celebrate the gift of flowers in your life by making these unique floral arrangements that are "frozen" in time.

Level: Moderately easy

Time involved: Two to three hours

Materials:

> Newspaper or plastic
>
> Latex gloves and protective clothing
>
> Glazing dip
>
> Disposable cup
>
> One dozen dried roses or summer flowers with stems
>
> Glass vase (Use one with a wide opening and wide base for best results.)
>
> Decorative glass pieces or marbles (optional)
>
> Floral-arranging gel
>
> Saucepan of hot water

1. Cover your work area with newspapers or plastic. Put on protective clothing and gloves. Pour the glazing dip into the disposable cup to the depth of the size of the roses. Hold the flower by the stem and dip the head completely into the glazing dip. Raise the flower over the cup and allow the excess dip to run off. Hold the flower upside down for several minutes until it is no longer dripping. Place the flower in the vase and allow it to dry. Repeat this step with the remaining flowers.

2. Once the flowers are dry, remove them from the vase. If there are any dried drips on the flowers, you can cut them off with scissors.

3. Prepare the vase by adding the decorative glass chips or marbles to the bottom if desired. Place the unopened bottle of floral-arranging gel into a pan of hot water until the gel liquefies. Carefully pour the gel into the vase. Arrange your roses in the gel and allow it to solidify.

That's the Spirit

Remembering the sacrifices of so many brave men and women to win our freedom and training our children to also remember is our sacred duty.

Remember the days of long ago; think about the generations past. Ask your father and he will inform you. Inquire of your elders, and they will tell you.

—Deuteronomy 32:7

This craft should only be done with children under strict supervision. Be sure to protect your work area with newspapers and wear protective clothing when working with floral-arranging gel and dipping glaze. Work in a well-ventilated area and avoid inhaling the fumes. The mediums are flammable, so store the bottles in a cool area away from flames or sparks. As with all crafting supplies, keep them out of the reach of children or pets.

Guess What?

Memorial Day is an official holiday celebrated on the last Monday in May in most of the United States. It is a time set aside to honor the nation's service personnel killed during wartime. This holiday, marked by parades, memorial ceremonies, and the decoration of gravesites, was first observed on May 30, 1868. It was then that, upon the order of John Alexander Logan, flowers were placed on the graves of the Union and Confederate soldiers at Arlington National Cemetery. The South originally refused to honor the date until after World War I when the holiday changed from honoring just those who died in the Civil War to honoring those who died in any war.

Country Candleholders

Light up your picnic table with this quaint set of country-style candleholders.

Level: Easy

Time involved: One to two hours

Materials:

Newspaper

2 (3-inch) clay flowerpots

2 (2-inch) clay flowerpots

2 (1½-inch) clay flowerpots

Red, white, blue, and gold craft paints

Paintbrushes

Two wooden candleholders (You can find these packaged in bags in the wood section of craft stores.)

Glue gun

Clear acrylic finish spray

Two red, white, or blue candles

A candleholder designed from clay flowerpots.

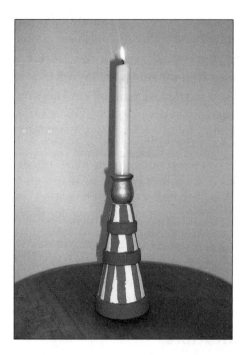

1. Cover your work area with newspapers. Paint the rims of all of the pots blue. Paint the remainder of each pot white and allow these to dry. (You do not have to paint the inside of these pots.) Paint red stripes vertically on each pot. Paint the wooden candleholders gold and allow to dry.

2. Using the glue gun, glue the 2-inch pots to the bottom of the 4-inch pots. Then glue the 1½-inch clay pots to the bottom of the 2-inch pots. Glue the wooden candleholder to the bottom of the 1½-inch pot. Spray the candlesticks with clear acrylic finish spray and allow to dry.

3. Place a red, white, or blue candle in each holder.

Fabulous Fourth

The Fourth of July celebrates the birth of the United States. It's a time for enjoying fireworks, family picnics and vacations, and the freedom to do whatever makes us happy. Share a few moments of this time with your family or friends working on these patriotic projects.

Guess What?

The Battle of Baltimore, fought in 1814 as part of the War of 1812, inspired the writing of "The Star Spangled Banner." President James Madison sent Francis Scott Key, a prominent lawyer, to obtain the release from the British of his old friend, Dr. Beanes. It was during this time that the battle of Baltimore was fought. Key was standing downriver from the battle and put the events into a poem. Despite several attempts, the British were unable to take the city, and they departed from Baltimore. Key wrote the poem to be sung to the old English tune "To Anacreon in Heaven." "The Star Spangled Banner" grew in popularity, and in 1931, Congress declared it the National Anthem.

Four-Star Service

Impress your family and friends by serving refreshments on this serving tray with a flag motif. You might want to make one of these for a hostess gift for that upcoming Fourth-of-July barbecue.

Serving refreshments on a red, white, and blue tray.

Level: Moderately easy

Time involved: Three to four hours, plus overnight to dry

Materials:

Newspaper or plastic

Unfinished wooden serving tray (You can find this in the wood section of craft stores.)

Red craft paint

Paintbrushes

Red, white, and blue bandana or material

Pen

Scissors

Decoupage finish

Varnish

Thin white ribbon or trim

Glue gun

1. Cover your work area with newspapers or plastic. Paint the entire wooden tray red. Add a second coat if necessary. Allow this to dry.

2. Place the bandana or material on a flat surface. Lay the tray on top of the material, and trace around the tray with a pen. (If necessary, iron the bandana or material before using it.) Cut the tray shape out of the bandana or material.

3. Place a light coat of decoupage finish on the wrong side of the material. Place this on the inside of the wooden tray and smooth in place with your fingers. When this is completely dry, brush a light coat of decoupage finish over the entire project. Repeat with a second coat. Allow this to dry.

4. Paint the wooden tray with a coat of varnish on the sides and inside of the tray, covering over the fabric. Allow this to dry and then repeat on the bottom of the tray. Allow the tray to dry overnight.

5. Cut the ribbon or trim to form a border inside the tray around the fabric design. Using a glue gun, glue the ribbon onto the tray. If desired, you can glue a border of ribbon around the painted outsides of the tray.

You can customize a hostess tray by cutting several designs out of fabric and using decoupage finish to attach them to the tray. You might want to consider adapting this tray to other holidays by using the appropriate holiday theme. For example, you could use material with hearts for Valentine's Day, or pumpkins and autumn leaves for Thanksgiving.

Guess What?

It's not certain where the image of Uncle Sam originated. One theory is that Uncle Sam represented Samual Wilson. During the War of 1812, Wilson, owner of a meat-packing plant, sent provisions to U.S. soldiers in large barrels. These barrels were stamped with the letters "U.S.," which some jokingly suggested stood for "Uncle Sam" Wilson. Through this link to the army, Uncle Sam became a symbol of the federal government.

Ice-Cream Fantasy

Ahh! the beginning of the summer vacation season. Kids are excited to get a break from busy school schedules (and so are their parents). It's a great time to relax and spend some time outdoors renewing creative energies. Kids and adults alike can agree that a favorite sign of the summer season is hearing the ice-cream truck come down the street and the day the ice-cream stands open. You can make your own rendition of this crowd-pleaser out of a few simple ingredients.

Level: Easy

Time involved: One to two hours

Materials:

Newspaper or plastic

Gold acrylic paint

Disposable cup

Paintbrush

3-inch-wide 4-inch-high clay pot

3-inch clay saucer

Glue gun

3-inch ball candle

A candle that looks good enough to eat!

1. Cover your work area with newspapers or plastic. Pour a small amount of gold paint in the disposable cup. Paint a gold line along the rim of the pot. Paint a second gold line around the bottom of the rim. Paint a pattern of triangles on the bottom of the pot (see illustration).

2. Paint the saucer gold. Using the glue gun, glue the bottom of the saucer to the top of the pot.

3. Place the ball candle in the saucer. The saucer will catch any drips that may occur when the candle is burning.

Creating the ice-cream-cone effect.

(Melissa LeBon)

Labor of Love

Labor Day, celebrated the first Monday in September, is an official holiday designated to honor the American working class. Free industry and a dedicated labor force helped to make America the great nation that it is today. Labor Day also signals the end of summer vacation and a return to school for the kids. Help savor this final summer holiday by spending some time with the kids designing eye-catching craft projects.

Guess What?

You might celebrate Labor Day by having a picnic with your friends and family, but are you aware of the reasons behind this celebration? (No, I'm not talking about Labor Day Sales!) Labor Day, celebrated on the first Monday in September, is a creation of the labor movement dedicated to the achievements of American workers. The first Monday in September was selected as the official Labor Day holiday in 1884.

Aquatic Art

If you're into tropical fish and plants, then this project is perfect for you. The aquatic garden is easy to assemble, and it makes a beautiful decoration for a den or an office.

A lovely home for a beautiful fish.

Level: Moderately easy

Time involved: One to two hours

Materials:

> 1 (10¾-inch) vase (Craft stores sell these vases, and some will include the saucer for free. I found all the necessary ingredients for this project at a garden shop.)
>
> 1 (4-inch) plastic saucer
>
> 1 pack of decorative rocks or marbles
>
> 1 water-loving plant (such as a peace lily)
>
> Scissors
>
> 1 gallon bottled water
>
> 1 Beta fish (or Japanese fighting fish)
>
> 1 yard red, white, and blue ribbon

1. Rinse off the vase, saucer, and rocks or marbles with water and set them aside.

2. Remove the plant from the pot and thoroughly rinse all the roots. You may have to soak them to get them clean. Trim the ends of the roots so that they are about four inches long.

3. Using scissors, cut a two-inch hole in the bottom of the plastic saucer. Work the roots through the hole. Place a two-inch layer of rocks or marbles in the bottom of the vase. Fill the vase with bottled water to about three inches below the neck of the vase.

4. Place the plastic bag containing the fish in the vase for about an hour to acclimate it to the temperature of the water. The water should be around room temperature. Carefully float the fish out of the bag and fill the vase to about one inch from the top with more bottled water. There should be about a one-inch space between the bottom of the saucer and the water level for the fish to breathe. Do not use tap water as it contains chlorine that is harmful to the fish.

5. Work the roots from the saucer into the vase and allow the saucer to rest on the lip of the vase. Add decorative rocks to the saucer to hold it in place.

6. Tie a red, white, and blue bow around the top of the vase.

That's the Spirit

"Work hard and cheerfully at whatever you do, as though you were working for the Lord rather than for people. Remember that the Lord will give you an inheritance as your reward, and the Master you are serving is Christ." (Colossians 3:23–24) How different would our workdays be if we started each one acknowledging the truths of these verses?

Place the vase in indirect sunlight and keep it in a warm spot (room temperature), out of drafts. Carefully lift the saucer from the vase to feed the fish.

Beta fish or Japanese fighting fish are aggressive fish that like to live alone. If you put two together in a bowl, they'll fight with each other. You can feed your fish prepared fish pellets from a pet shop and give it shrimp brine and dried blood worms for a treat. Change about 25 percent of the fish's water each week by adding bottled water that is the same temperature as the water the fish is residing in. If necessary, trim the roots of the plant if they become too long.

Antique Designs

If you're cooped up on a rainy Labor Day weekend, you might want to try making these antique vases or candleholders to brighten up your dinner table.

Level: Easy

Time involved: Two to three hours

Materials:

> Newspaper or plastic
>
> Glue gun
>
> Small objects with a raised surface such as pasta shapes, cereal, beads, cord, buttons, and bottle caps
>
> Glass bottles
>
> White glue
>
> Aluminum foil
>
> Black tempera paint
>
> Liquid detergent
>
> Disposable cup
>
> Paintbrush

1. Cover your work area with newspapers or plastic. Using a glue gun, glue the raised objects onto the bottle, creating an interesting design. Be sure that you cover the entire surface fairly well. Allow to dry.

2. Cover a small area of the bottle with white glue. Using small pieces of aluminum foil, cover the glued area and press the foil into all the crevices. Don't worry if the foil splits or gets a hole in it; it will be covered by the black paint. Continue to add the foil until the entire bottle is covered.

3. Make a solution of two parts black tempera and one part liquid detergent. Paint this mixture onto the bottle, a small area at a time, making sure to get it into all the cracks. Use a small piece of crumpled newspaper to buff the black paint off of the high areas of your bottle. The black paint should remain in the cracks, with the raised areas free of paint, giving the bottle an antique look.

Add flowers or a candle to the bottle, and place it on your picnic table to light up your Labor Day feast.

Steps to making an antique vase or candleholder.

(Melissa LeBon)

Food, Glorious Food!

Backyard barbecues are the name of the game for summer holiday weekends. If you're throwing a holiday bash, you'll want to check out these ideas for the perfect picnic foods.

Grilled chicken-salad sandwiches make a delicious summer picnic lunch. The next time you make chicken on the grill, try adding an extra breast or two to make chicken salad. Marinate the chicken first in a vinaigrette salad dressing for two hours before grilling.

The grilled chicken is great on a Caesar salad for dinner, and the extra pieces can be chopped up for chicken salad for your picnic lunch the next day. Add ½ cup chopped celery, ¼ cup chopped onion, ¼ cup chopped red pepper, and about ⅓ cup mayonnaise to the chicken, and mix well. Season with salt and pepper to taste.

Fruit Fantasy

When it's too hot to eat anything else, fruit is a great choice to boost your energy. Try making this decorative and delicious watermelon basket for your next summer event.

Level: Moderately difficult

Time involved: One to two hours

Family Ties

Summertime is a great time to connect with extended family. Use vacation time to visit with family members. Plan or attend a family reunion. It is important that your children get to know their roots.

A family tree can wither if nobody tends its roots.

—Unknown

Ingredients:

Whole seedless watermelon (Choose one that sits straight on its underbelly. A ripe watermelon should have a whitish-yellow underbelly where it was lying on the ground.)

Cantaloupe

Honeydew

Berries (strawberries, raspberries, blueberries)

Green seedless grapes

8-oz. package cream cheese

7-oz. jar marshmallow whip

Equipment:

    Pencil

    Sharp knife

    Large bowl

    Melon-ball utensil

    Large spoon or scoop

    Paring knife

    Electric mixer or food processor

Cutting out a watermelon fruit basket.

(Melissa LeBon)

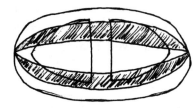

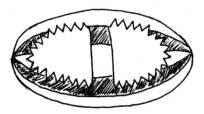

1. Wash the outside of the watermelon. Draw the design of the basket on the top-side (green side) of the watermelon with a pencil. You should have two triangular shapes, one on each side of the melon, with a two-inch strip for the handle in the middle (see illustration).

2. Cut the two triangles out, being careful not to knick the edges of the handle. Pry the two triangles out of the watermelon with your hands and place them in a bowl.

3. Using the melon-ball utensil, begin scraping out the watermelon using a quick twist of the utensil to form a ball. If you use a seeded watermelon, you'll have to remove the seeds from the balls with your fingers. (I always use a seedless watermelon for this reason.) Make as many watermelon balls as you can, and then scrape the remainder of the watermelon fruit out of the skin with a spoon. Discard or eat the watermelon scraps. Make balls out of any watermelon attached to the two triangles that you cut out. Discard the skin.

4. Using a paring knife, cut a notched edge into the edge of the basket as shown. Make one cut on an angle to the left, and a second cut on an angle to the right to form a notch, and repeat around the perimeter of the basket. (This step is not as hard to do as it seems.) You can continue to notch the handle if desired, but it looks fine un-notched, and you'll minimize your chances of cutting through the handle by mistake if you leave the edges smooth.

5. Once you've notched your basket, place the watermelon balls in the basket.

6. Cut the cantaloupe in half and remove the seeds with a spoon. Use the melon-ball utensil to make cantaloupe balls. Repeat this step with the honeydew, so you have three different melon balls. Place the balls in the watermelon basket and mix them together. Wash berries and grapes and add to melon.

7. Using a mixer or food processor, mix the cream cheese and marshmallow whip in a bowl. Place the mixture in a small bowl to use as a dip for the fruit.

Artichoke Dip

Artichoke dip is so simple to make and yet it gets rave reviews from company. All you need is a food processor and three ingredients to make this mouthwatering dip.

Level: Easy

Time involved: Half to one hour

Ingredients:

Can of whole artichoke hearts (You can find this in the canned-vegetable section of the supermarket.)

10-ounce brick white mild or medium cheddar cheese (You could use a 10-ounce package of shredded cheddar cheese instead.)

½ cup mayonnaise

Nonstick cooking spray

Crackers

Equipment:

Food processor

Mixing bowl

Small ovenproof baking dish

1. Preheat the oven to 350°F. Open the can of artichoke hearts and drain them, discarding the liquid. Place the artichoke hearts in a food processor and surge the power until the hearts are cut into chunks (not mushy). Place in a mixing bowl.

2. Cut the brick of cheese into chunks and shred in the food processor. Remove to the mixing bowl. (If using shredded cheese, add now.) Add ½ cup mayonnaise to the mixture and stir thoroughly.

3. Spray the baking dish with nonstick cooking spray. Add the artichoke mixture and pat it down with a spoon. Bake the mixture for approximately 20 minutes or until melted and golden brown. Serve with crackers.

Low-fat butter and mayonnaise have come a long way; unfortunately, although their taste has improved, they don't always hold up well in recipes. I tried using nonfat mayonnaise in the artichoke dip, and it was a disaster. The dip had a dry, as opposed to a creamy, texture and it didn't brown well. Along the same lines, substituting low-fat butter or margarine in recipes that call for real butter or margarine doesn't usually work, especially when the dishes are baked (such as cakes, cookies, and breads).

Giving Thanks

What is *your* fondest memory of a Thanksgiving celebration? For many, Thanksgiving conjures up thoughts of succulent roasted turkey, herb stuffing, buttery potatoes, and Mom's homemade pies. But Thanksgiving is more than just a day for feasting on rich, traditional foods. For most, Thanksgiving Day is spent with friends and relatives gathered around a table to give thanks for all the blessings of the past year.

The Thanksgiving tradition began with a group of people from England in the 1600s. At this time in history, a group of men and women known as Puritans were seeking religious freedom. They desired their own land where they could live as Englishmen and practice their faith in peace. They made a contract to sail to America on the *Mayflower*. One hundred two Pilgrims were aboard the ship and about half of these were children. After a long and difficult voyage, the ship landed on December 11, 1620, just off the coast of Cape Cod.

The Pilgrims' first winter was an extremely harsh one. Only about 50 of the original travelers survived. Half of these were children and only four were women. They managed to survive the harsh winters with the aid of Native American friends who helped them farm and hunt for food. In 1676, with their community fully established, the governing council of Charlestown, Massachusetts, proclaimed June 26 to be an official day of Thanksgiving.

Nowadays, people celebrate Thanksgiving on the fourth Thursday in November. If you're the person in charge of creating a special Thanksgiving for your family, you'll want to check out the craft and food ideas in this chapter that will make your celebration another reason to be thankful.

Guess What?

It's not certain whether turkey was served at the first Thanksgiving feast, but we do know that the menu included wildfowl, sea bass and cod, cornmeal, fruits and vegetables, and five deer provided by the Native Americans. There probably wasn't pumpkin pie, as the settlers had run out of flour, but boiled pumpkin and wild berries may have topped off the meal.

Giving Thanks

Many symbols of Thanksgiving are centered on the bounty of the harvest. You won't regret taking the time to dress up your home with these creative symbols of the season.

Autumn Wreath

Nothing creates a welcoming atmosphere more completely than a lovely seasonal wreath hung on your front door. This wreath is relatively easy to make and will make the vibrant fall colors come alive in your home.

A lovely wreath to welcome your guests.

Level: Moderately easy

Time involved: Two to three hours

Materials:

> Large bunch of brown eucalyptus
>
> Large grapevine wreath
>
> Wire
>
> Wire cutters
>
> Bunch of silk fall-colored flowers
>
> Glue gun
>
> 3 yards thick ribbon in a matching color
>
> 24 small pine cones

1. Place the eucalyptus branches around the grapevine wreath, covering the top of the wreath, and wire them into place.

2. Make a row of about 12 fall flowers on the bottom of the wreath, leaving space in between some of them to place pine cones. Wire or glue these in place.

3. Make a bow out of the ribbon. Wire the ribbon onto the top of the wreath. Then wire three or four flowers onto each side of the bow.

4. Glue the pine cones in a random pattern onto the wreath. Be sure to glue some in between the flowers and at the beginning and end of the stretch of flowers. The sides of the wreath should show some eucalyptus.

That's the Spirit

"Give thanks to the Lord, for he is good! His faithful love endures forever." (1 Chronicles 16:34) Every day should be a thanksgiving day for the family whose God is the Lord.

Display your wreath on a door or above a mantle to welcome your guests to your home.

Turkey Tags

Make one of these cute little turkeys for each guest at your holiday table. Have a few extras made up and ready to personalize for last-minute additions. Add the date and your family name to the back, and your guests have a memento of their time with you.

A lovely invitation to the Thanksgiving feast.

Level: Easy

Time involved: One to two hours

Materials:

> 7 (2-inch) oval wooden pieces (*Woodsies*)
>
> Brown, red, green, yellow, blue, and orange craft paints
>
> Paintbrushes
>
> Foam plate
>
> Flat 3-inch wooden circle (These can be found in bags in the wood section of a craft store.)
>
> 2 (1½-inch) oval wooden pieces
>
> Small triangular wooden piece for beak
>
> Glue gun
>
> Plastic eyes
>
> Black calligraphy marker
>
> Clear acrylic finish spray

1. Paint six of the two-inch wooden ovals each a different color: red, yellow, green, blue, orange, and brown. Paint the remaining two-inch wooden oval and the circle brown. Paint the two 1½-inch oval pieces orange and the triangular piece red. Paint a second coat if necessary. Allow these to dry.

2. Glue the six wooden ovals (feathers) onto the back of the top half of the circle. Glue the brown oval piece in the middle of the circle to form a head. Glue the triangle nose onto the head. Then glue the two smaller oval pieces flat onto the bottom of the body to form feet that will make the turkey stand up.

3. Glue two plastic eyes on the head. Write the name of the guest on the bottom of the circle using a calligraphy marker.

4. Spray the project with clear acrylic finish spray and allow it to dry for several hours.

def·i·ni·tion Plain and Simple

Woodsies are a trademarked name for craft wood that is cut into assorted shapes and sizes and packaged in bags. You can find them in the wood section of craft stores, and they usually include suggestions for using them. For example, there is a bag of Woodsies that is designed for making animals, which includes ovals, circles, sticks, ears, noses, and so on. There are also craft books you can buy to get ideas for using these wooden pieces in special projects. Setting out several bags of Woodsies, some paint markers, and tacky glue could provide hours of entertainment at a kids' sleepover.

Colonial Crafts

Colonial America is a tradition-rich time in our country's history. Your family can learn a lot from these brave people who endured hardship in order to worship God and the Native Americans who helped them survive in a new and hostile land.

Guess What?

The pilgrims had not intended to settle in Plymouth. Back in England, the Puritans heard about the thriving colony of Jamestown, Virginia, and had applied and received a charter to found a plantation near this colony at the mouth of the Hudson River. However, violent storms blew the *Mayflower* off course. Instead, they landed far north of their destination, just off the coast of Cape Cod. Realizing that their original agreement as a group was legal only in Virginia, the Pilgrims drafted the Mayflower Compact before debarking from the ship. This agreement fashioned laws for the good of the new colony and established a lasting form of government.

Handmade Beads

Native Americans are superb artisans and they pass down their knowledge and skill from generation to generation. You and your family will enjoy practicing your artistic skill making beautiful beads to string for a necklace. You may want to design beads that represent God's blessings in your life. Then as you string them, you and your family can count your blessings.

A handmade necklace of colorful beads.

Level: Moderately easy

Time involved: One to two hours

Materials:

> Suede lace (⅛ inch), 1 yard per necklace
>
> Sculpey baking clay in a variety of colors
>
> Skewer or toothpick
>
> Scissors

1. Let everyone's creativity overflow! Sculpey clay can be molded into any shape or size of bead. It comes in rich colors that can be combined to make beautiful patterns. By kneading colors together, you can create new colors. If left out too long, it will start to air dry so you may want to store what you're not using in a plastic bag until you need it.

2. After beads are formed, use a skewer to create a hole through the center of each bead. You can use a toothpick, but you will need to wiggle the toothpick around to make the hole large enough for the suede lace to fit through it. A skewer seems to be just about the right dimension and its extra length allows you to pierce longer beads.

3. Place beads on a cookie sheet and bake according to the directions on the Sculpey package (usually 275°F for about 15 minutes per ¼-inch thickness).

4. After the beads have cooled, you and your family can string them onto the suede lace. You might want to knot the lace between beads for spacing and to add to the design.

5. When a necklace is complete, knot the two ends together. The necklace should be long enough to slip over the head.

Caution: Sculpey clay is so much fun that you might end up making all sorts of things besides beads! Even my pre-teen and teenage kids enjoy this activity. Your bead session may turn into hours and hours of creative family fun.

Spicy Pomanders

Help your children make these wonderfully scented *pomanders* as Thanksgiving Day gifts or to hang about your home so that everyone who enters is welcomed with a spicy aroma. These need to be made two to three weeks in advance of the holidays.

Try these spicy aromatic treats.

Level: Easy

Time involved: Under an hour to make; two to three weeks to dry

Materials:

> Whole lemon, orange, tangerine, or apple
>
> Whole cloves
>
> Whole cinnamon sticks
>
> Toothpicks
>
> Rubber bands or yarn
>
> Thin cotton fabric or tulle
>
> Ribbon or raffia
>
> Silk leaves (optional)

1. Use toothpicks to poke holes in the fruit, keeping the holes fairly close together. Instead of random pokes, try a pattern of rows.

2. Insert a whole clove into each hole in the fruit.

3. Wrap each pomander in a piece of cotton cloth or tulle (approximately eight inches square). Secure the corners with a rubber band or yarn.

> **def·i·ni·tion Plain and Simple**
>
> A **pomander** is a mixture of aromatic substances balled together. Early Americans used pomanders to scent clothes and linens. They also believed that the aromas were a safeguard against infection.

4. Hang fruit in the open air for two to three weeks until the fruit hardens. Every few days, turn the pomanders upside down to prevent the fruit from spoiling.

5. Remove the dried fruit from their coverings and accent with ribbon or raffia, silk leaves, and whole cinnamon sticks. Add a small card with this prayer: May our lives be a sweet fragrance presented by Christ to God (from 2 Corinthians 2:15).

6. Your aromatic pomanders may be placed in drawers or closets, hung in the car, or given as gifts.

Kiddy Krafts

The Thanksgiving holiday is a wonderful time to teach kids to be grateful for all their blessings. You could spend some time with them working together on these projects to help them appreciate the gifts of family, friends, and community.

Counting Your Blessings

Give special meaning to your Thanksgiving celebration by helping your kids create this poster that expresses what they are thankful for in their lives.

Level: Easy

Time involved: One to two hours

Materials:

> Magazines
>
> Scissors
>
> Markers
>
> Poster board
>
> White glue
>
> Thanksgiving stickers

1. Sit down with your kids and help them look through magazines to find pictures that express what they are thankful for. Cut out the pictures.

2. Prepare the poster board by writing the words "What I Am Thankful For" at the top of the poster board. Glue the pictures onto the poster board in an attractive pattern. Use the markers to label each picture and to fill in the spaces with color. Add a Scripture verse with a thankful theme at the bottom.

3. Decorate the poster board with Thanksgiving stickers. This can be an ongoing project that you can add to over the holiday season as more pictures are found.

If you haven't already done this, Thanksgiving would be a great time to volunteer your family to work at a local soup kitchen or for a feed-a-friend program. It's an eye opener for kids to see how fortunate they really are to have a stable home life and all the blessings God provides.

Handprint Turkey

It's easy to make simple turkeys out of handprints. You might want to make a family of turkeys using the hands of everyone in your family. These cute turkeys would make nice place cards for the dinner table.

That's the Spirit

Speaking Scripture is a wonderful way to give thanks. Read together these verses from Psalm 136 as part of your Thanksgiving celebration.

Give thanks to the Lord, for he is good!
His faithful love endures forever. (verse 1)

Give thanks to him who alone does mighty miracles.
His faithful love endures forever. (verse 4)

He gives food to every living thing.
His faithful love endures forever. (verse 25)

Give thanks to the God of heaven.
His faithful love endures forever. (verse 26)

Level: Easy

Time involved: One to two hours

Materials:

> Poster board
>
> Markers or crayons
>
> White glue
>
> Feathers
>
> Plastic eyes
>
> Scissors
>
> Magnet (optional)

1. Let the kids trace the hands of each member of the family onto the poster board. Color the handprint turkeys with a light brown marker or crayon.

2. Spread glue on the tails (fingers) of the turkeys. Glue a feather onto each finger (not on the thumb).

3. Glue an eye onto the heads (thumbs) of the turkeys. Draw red beaks protruding from the heads. Draw two orange legs on the bottom of each turkey.

4. Cut out the turkeys. Write the names of the family members on the front of the turkey using a black marker.

5. If desired, glue a magnet onto the back of the turkeys and arrange them on the refrigerator.

If using these as place cards, cut out a small piece of poster board and fold it in half to create a stand. Glue the turkey onto the front of the poster board and place it on the table. You could let family members take turns at writing on the turkey cards to tell each person why they're thankful for him or her.

You can also make a wreath out of the kids' handprints. Cut a large wreath shape from poster board and attach the handprint cut-outs, adding holiday symbols (colored leaves, pumpkins, corn) in between. This craft can be adapted to other seasons as well. You also might want to write messages on the handprints such as: "Things I'm Thankful For" for Thanksgiving, or "The Reasons I Love You" for Valentine's Day.

Food, Glorious Food

You can't forget the food when planning your Thanksgiving celebration. Whether you do a traditional turkey dinner or like to experiment with menus, you won't go wrong by checking out these recipes.

Crunchy Cranberries

Don't just shake cranberry sauce out of a can this year; make your own fresh cranberry relish for your Thanksgiving Day meal. This delicious recipe is a favorite of Dr. Carol Taylor of Georgetown, Washington, D.C., and has been a staple of the Taylor family menu for years.

Level: Easy

Time involved: Half to one hour

Ingredients:

1 bag fresh cranberries

1 orange

¾ cup sugar

½ cup walnuts (optional)

Equipment:

> Food processor
>
> Bowl
>
> Mixing spoon

1. Wash the cranberries and allow them to dry. Grind up the cranberries in a food processor, a small amount at a time, and remove them to the mixing bowl. Do not overprocess the cranberries to the point where they are mushy.
2. Wash the orange and cut it into quarters. Remove any seeds. Grind the orange (peel and all) in the food processor. Add this to the mixing bowl.
3. Add sugar and walnuts, if desired, to the mixture and stir until well blended.
4. Refrigerate the cranberry relish overnight for the best taste and color.

Mom's Pumpkin Pie

No one makes pumpkin pie like Mom does. Well, now you can, if you follow this easy recipe supplied by my mom, Mildred Taylor, of Pine Grove, Pennsylvania.

Level: Moderately easy

Time involved: One to two hours

Ingredients:

> 2 eggs
>
> 1¾ cups pumpkin (Mom uses her own neck pumpkins, peeled, cut, and boiled, but you can substitute canned pumpkin—the 29-ounce size.)
>
> ¾ cup sugar (use ½ white sugar and ½ brown sugar)
>
> ½ tsp. salt
>
> 1 tsp. cinnamon
>
> ½ tsp. ginger
>
> ½ tsp. cloves
>
> 1⅔ cup evaporated milk
>
> 1 TB. molasses
>
> Ready-made pie crust

Equipment:

> Electric mixer
>
> 9-inch pie pan

1. Preheat the oven to 425°F. Place two eggs in the mixer and beat slightly. Add the pumpkin and mix well. Add the dry ingredients and blend together until well mixed. Blend in the evaporated milk and molasses.
2. Make a crust in the pie pan following the manufacturer's directions for a pre-pared crust. Pour the pumpkin mixture into the pan.
3. Bake for 15 minutes and then turn the heat to 350°F. Bake at this temperature for 45 minutes. The pumpkin pie is done when the tip of a knife inserted in the center comes out clean and the pumpkin mixture is solidified.

You can avoid having a burnt crust when baking pies in the oven for long periods of time by covering the crust with aluminum foil after it turns a golden brown color. You can also buy metal piecrust shields online, from mail-order catalogs, or in a dis-count store, which you can simply place over the crust to keep it from getting too dark. The shields that I've used are made by Betty Crocker.

Savory Stuffing

You can make your stuffing from scratch without a lot of hassle if you use prepared seasoned bread-stuffing cubes. You'll get rave reviews from your family for this spe-cial stuffing recipe sent to me by Dr. Robert Barnet of Reno, Nevada.

Level: Moderately easy

Time involved: One to two hours

Ingredients:

> 2 (16-oz.) bags seasoned bread cubes
>
> 1 cup corn meal
>
> 2 cups bread crumbs
>
> ½ cup chopped walnuts
>
> ½ cup white raisins

1 tsp. chopped dry or fresh sage

1 tsp. chopped dry or fresh thyme

1 tsp. salt

½ tsp. pepper

1 cup celery (especially tips and leaves) cut into ½-inch lengths

1 medium-size onion, chopped

4 garlic cloves, chopped

10 to 12 small mushrooms, sliced (These can be added fresh or sautéed in olive oil first.)

1 cooking apple, cored and sliced into thick pieces

1 egg

1 stick butter, melted

1 or 2 cups chicken broth

Equipment:

Large mixing bowl

Mixing spoon

Cooking spray

13 × 9-inch baking dish (optional)

Mix the ingredients together in the mixing bowl in the order listed. Use enough chicken broth to make the mixture soft and moist, but not sticky (according to your preference). Stuff the turkey with the mixture or place it in a baking dish sprayed with cooking oil. Add some drippings from the turkey and bake this at 350°F for 30 minutes.

Chapter

16

Christmas

Christmas is a unique holiday, celebrated in many different ways by people throughout the world. But one common thread is that Christmas celebrates a spirit of giving, represented by God's best gift—the birth of his Son Jesus Christ. Like most other families, you probably spend time together during this season decorating your home, buying and wrapping presents, and preparing food for the festivities. Throughout the festivities, you can be sharing traditions and lessons with your family that will strengthen your relationships and strengthen your walk with God.

Christmas vacation is a perfect opportunity to take some time from the hustle and bustle of the season and create your own version of goodwill on Earth. Make a date with your loved ones to try out some of the crafts in this chapter. You can get ahead of the game by substituting a relaxing session of craft-making for a hectic shopping trip to the mall. The people on your gift list will love receiving your handcrafted treasures, and you will be making lasting memories for your family.

Christmas Creations

Plenty of Christmas symbols can be crafted into stylish decorations for your home. Check out the following crafts to do together as a family.

Countdown to Christmas

With this Christmas calendar, you and your loved ones can enjoy the daily surprises under each door as you wait to welcome the Christ child into your home. Melissa LeBon, of Mountaintop, Pennsylvania, designed this clever house-shape Advent calendar to count down the days to Christmas.

Level: Moderately easy

Time involved: Two to three hours

Materials:

> 12×18-inch foam sheets: one green, one brown, one red, two white
>
> Scissors
>
> Exacto knife
>
> Cutting board
>
> Glue gun
>
> Rub-on numbers (½ inch or ¾ inch)
>
> Old Christmas cards

1. Using scissors, cut two pieces of white foam sheet 13×11 inches. Cut two pieces of brown foam sheet 12×7 inches. Cut the sides of the brown foam sheet on an angle to resemble a roof, and make two chimneys on top as shown. Glue the brown roofs onto the top edges of the white foam sheets to form two houses.

2. Cut a rectangle out of the red foam sheet that is 3×5 inches to make the front door. Glue the door onto the white foam house. Place the house on a cutting board and cut around the top, bottom, and right edges of the door using an Exacto knife to make a door that opens. Make a 2-inch wreath out of the green

foam sheet and glue it to the door. Cut a small red ribbon out of the red foam sheet and glue it to the wreath as shown.

3. Make hedges out of the green foam sheet and glue them to the bottom of the house. If desired, use a little *snow texture paint* on the tops of the shrubbery and the rooftop to give the effect of snow.

4. Cut 10 brown boxes (doors), approximately 1½ inches square, out of the brown foam sheet. You can mix up the sizes and make different shapes if you desire. Glue these doors onto the roof of the house form containing the front door. Place the house on a cutting board and cut around the top, bottom, and right side of the boxes with the Exacto knife to form doors that open.

5. Cut pictures out of old Christmas cards that fit the size of the doors. Glue the pictures onto the back of the foam sheet so that they are visible when the doors are opened. Put a picture of the Christ child behind the front door, which will be numbered 24, to be opened Christmas Eve.

6. Repeat steps 4 and 5, making 13 green foam sheet boxes and placing them on the white section of the house. If desired, you can use a marker to make frames around the boxes, to resemble windows or shutters. Doors can also be placed in the shrubs around the house.

7. Place the finished house over the second house, lining up the roof and sides. Glue the two pieces together.

8. Put the numbers 1 through 24 on the outside of the doors. The number 24 should be on the front door. Number the doors in random order to make the "hunt" for the next number more interesting.

def·i·ni·tion

Plain and Simple

You can find **snow texture paint** in a craft store. It's usually packaged in a small jar and can be applied to a craft with a paintbrush, sponge, or spatula. This stucco-effect paint is perfect for winter projects that require a snow effect. It can also be mixed with colored paints to create a unique textured surface.

For added interest, make a production out of opening your calendar each day by gathering the family together and taking turns opening the doors. You might want to enhance this activity by gluing Christmas symbols, such as a star, angel, tree, or candle, behind some doors. When those doors are opened, share the meaning of these Christian symbols and how thinking about them will help prepare our hearts for Christmas.

*Designing and cutting out
your Christmas calendar.*

(Melissa LeBon)

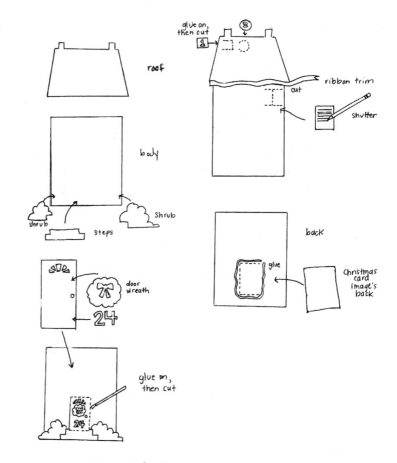

Guess What?

Here are some explanations for Christmas symbols to share with your family:

- **Angel.** The angels brought the Good News of Jesus' birth first to Mary, and then to the shepherds. Angels remind us to share the Good News of Christmas.
- **Star.** A special star showed the wise men how to find the baby Jesus. God wants us to shine like stars at Christmas to point others to him.
- **Tree.** The tree always points up to heaven and is always green, a sign of life and growth. God wants us to keep our focus on heaven and to always be growing in our Christian life.
- **Candle.** A candle gives light. Jesus is the light of the world. We can be a light to those around us who are in the darkness of sin.

Bath Ornament

There's nothing like a soothing scented bath to wash away the stress of the holidays. These ornaments filled with homemade bath salts are inexpensive and simple and sure to please anyone on your gift list.

Scent-sational bath ornaments.

Level: Easy

Time involved: One to two hours to make a dozen

Materials:

Epsom salts

Dry powdered milk

Essential oil (your choice of scent)

Plastic ornaments with removable tops

Bowl

Mixing spoon

Ribbon

Scissors

Small funnel (like you use to fill salt shakers)

Scotch tape

1. In a large bowl measure 1 cup Epsom salts with 1 cup powdered milk for every 3 to 4 ornaments. (Each ornament will hold about ½ cup bath salts depending on size of ornaments.) Add a few drops of essential oil. (Lavender, rose, and lemon are all nice.) Stir together with a spoon.

2. Take the tops off of the ornaments and using the funnel, fill the ornaments with the bath salt mixture.

3. Place a small piece of scotch tape over the opening before replacing the ornament top.

4. Tie a ribbon to the top of the ornament and add a gift tag. This recipe is so simple and so delightful that you might want to share the bath salts recipe on the tag. Make several different scents, mark them with a different color ribbon on each ornament, and arrange several in a small basket with tissue paper or filler for a nice gift for a teacher or friend. Or give individual ornaments to neighbors and co-workers.

That's the Spirit

A relaxed attitude lengthens life; jealousy rots it away.

—Proverbs 14:30

With all the emphasis on material things and the commercialism of Christmas, it is easy to be undone by stress and jealousy. Guard your heart and teach your family that Christmas is the season of giving, not getting.

Angelic Accents

Make these angels to hang on your tree or around your home as a reminder of the Good Tidings they brought to the world long ago. Use different-colored and different-textured doilies to create a flurry of angel designs. Try singing along to some "angelic" Christmas music ("Hark the Herald Angels Sing" or "Angels We Have Heard on High") while working on this family craft.

Level: Moderately easy

Time involved: One hour

Materials:

Doily

Scissors

Round peg clothespin

Glue gun

Round wooden head that fits over the top of a clothespin (You can find these in a craft store.)

Piece of white foam sheet

Silver and gold metallic pipe cleaners

Black fine-tip marker

A heavenly accent for your home.

1. Make a ¼-inch slit in the middle of the doily. Make another ¼-inch slit intersecting the first slit. Insert the clothespin into the slit and glue it just below the round knob of the clothespin to form the neck of the angel. Glue the bead head to the clothespin.

2. Cut a piece of white foam sheet 3½ × 2 inches. Glue the 3½-inch ends together to make a tube out of the foam sheet. Glue this tube to the top of the clothespin underneath the doily.

3. Cut two 2-inch pieces of gold pipe cleaner. Glue one around the neck of the angel and one around the waist of the angel, gathering the doily equally around the body.

Family Ties

If you see that your children's behavior is becoming less than "angelic," check your schedule. As parents, too often we try to cram so much into the holiday season that we wear our children out. No wonder they're cranky!

4. Make angel wings by bending and twisting a silver pipe cleaner as shown in the figure. Using a glue gun, glue the wings onto a piece of white foam sheet. Cut around the wings. Cut a piece of silver pipe cleaner 6 inches long and form a 1-inch diameter halo in one end. Bend the other end around the wings. Glue the wings and halo onto the back of the angel.

5. Twist a 6-inch piece of silver pipe cleaner around the body of the angel to form arms. Make a coil out of a 3-inch piece of gold pipe cleaner, and glue it to the top of the angel's head to form hair.

6. Make a face on the angel's bead head using a fine-tip marker.

The steps to assembling a doily angel.

(Melissa LeBon)

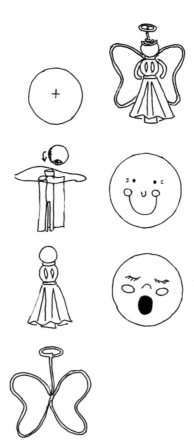

You can stand the angel up on its own or add an ornament hook to the back to hang it on your tree. Make a different version of an angel by substituting a large silk flower (magnolia or lily works well) for the doily. Omit the clothespin and foam tube and glue the bead head directly to the base of an upside-down single flower. Make the wings by twisting together two of the leaves and gluing them to the back of the angel. Add the hair and halo to your heavenly creation by following the directions for the doily angel.

Away in a Manger

Make a date with your kids to tell them the story of the first Christmas. Then spend the afternoon making your own nativity scene out of wooden spoons and craft sticks.

Try your hand at this basic design and then let the kids craft their own figures to add to the collection. You could extend the craft sticks at the bottom of the blackboard to add additional figures such as the three kings, shepherds, and barn animals.

A simple rendition of the Nativity scene.

Level: Easy

Time involved: One to two hours

Materials:

Paintbrushes

Brown, blue, yellow, white, and light-pink craft paints

Foam plate

Wooden spoons

Bag of assorted wooden pieces (ovals and squares)

Unfinished chalkboard

Wooden star

Clear acrylic finish spray

Glue gun

Eight yellow wooden craft sticks

Brown and black fine-tip markers

Plain and Simple

You can find **clear acrylic finish spray** in craft stores, discount stores, and home-improvement stores. This spray paint adds a shiny, protective finish to craft projects. It works well on wood, cardboard, clay, cement mosaics, and just about any hard, dry surface. It shouldn't be used on fabric, plaster, or paper. Clear acrylic finish spray makes a painted surface more permanent and protects the designs from wearing off with passing time.

1. Paint one wooden spoon (body) and two oval pieces (arms) with blue craft paint, leaving a small oval area at one end of each oval piece to make hands. Paint one wooden spoon and two oval pieces with brown craft paint, also leaving an area for hands. Make hands on the ends of the arms with light-pink craft paint. Paint a square wooden piece brown to form the base of the manger. Paint the frame of the blackboard brown and allow to dry.

Family Ties

Making a trip to see Christmas lights is a great family tradition no matter where you live. In Colorado, we all pile into the car and drive around to favorite spots. But when we visit Grandma and Grandpa in Arizona, we take a walking tour.

2. Paint two oval pieces the same size as the arms light pink (for Mary's and Joseph's heads). Paint a smaller oval piece light pink (for the baby's head) and allow to dry. Paint the top half of the two adult heads blue and brown to form veils.

3. Paint an oval piece slightly larger than the baby's head with white paint to form the body, and another larger oval piece with yellow paint to form the hay. Paint the wooden star yellow and allow to dry.

4. Spray all the painted pieces with clear acrylic finish spray and allow to dry.

5. Using a glue gun, glue the brown base of the manger to the bottom center of the blackboard. Glue the yellow oval to the square, the white oval to the yellow oval, and the pink oval to the white oval. Glue the brown and blue wooden spoons on either side of the manger. Glue the head and arms to the spoons.

That's the Spirit

"The life of the godly is full of light and joy." (Proverbs 13:9) Let all the lights at Christmas time bring you joy and remind you of the very best gift of all—new life in Jesus Christ.

6. Glue the yellow craft sticks onto the frame of the blackboard. You'll need two sticks for the top and bottom and one stick for each side. Glue two sticks into a peak on the top of the board. Glue the star on top of the peak.

7. Using a black fine-tip marker, make facial features on the heads. Use a brown marker to make hair on Mary's and the baby's heads.

Guess What?

The use of a star to symbolize Christmas dates back to the birth of Christ. It is said that an unusually bright star appeared quite miraculously in the eastern sky when Christ was born. This star led the magi (who were also astronomers) to believe that a great man was born that day. It also guided them to the birthplace (Bethlehem) of their newborn king. The star today symbolizes, within Christianity, high hopes and ideals for the future of humankind.

Crafty Containers

Instead of using store-bought paper on your presents this year, check out these craft ideas for unique finishing effects. You and your family will have hours of fun working on these clever gift-wrappings.

Stylish Stockings

"The stockings were hung by the chimney with care in hopes that St. Nicholas soon would be there …" Impress St. Nick with these elegant personalized stockings that will withstand the wear and tear of Christmas morning. You can make one for each member of your family or use one as a unique wrapping for a special gift.

Guess What?

Some say that the tradition of hanging stockings was started by St. Nicholas when he tried to help the daughters of an impoverished man attract husbands by providing them with dowries. According to the legend, St. Nicholas dropped bags of gold in the windows of the girls' rooms. One night one of the bags landed in a stocking that had been hung up to dry. Thus, the tradition of putting gifts in stockings was born.

Level: Moderately difficult

Time involved: One to two hours

Materials:

Two pieces of 24 × 20-inch Christmas quilted material

Ruler

Scissors

24 inches of 5-inch-wide lace

Straight pins

Sewing machine

Thread

Iron and ironing board

30 inches of matching trim

Glue gun

Green fabric paint in a squeeze bottle

Gold bell (optional)

Needle and thread

1. Place the two pieces of quilted material right sides together on a flat surface with the 20-inch length horizontal. Starting at the upper-left corner of the material, use a ruler to mark off 12 inches. At this mark, cut a straight, vertical line 15 inches long. Then make a horizontal cut to the right that is 8 inches long to form the foot area of the stocking. Make a second vertical cut 9 inches long to complete the foot area. Round off the corners of the foot area and heel area as shown (see illustration).

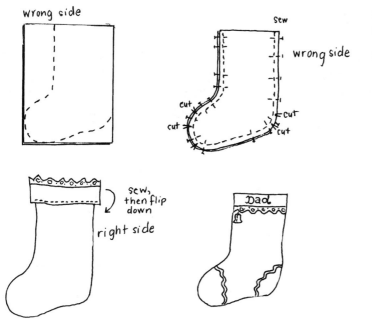

Cutting and sewing a
Christmas stocking.

(Melissa LeBon)

2. Cut two pieces of the lace 12 inches in length. Pin a piece of lace to the top of
    each stocking with the "right side" of the lace against the "wrong side" of the
    stocking material. Sew the lace along the tops of the stockings using a ½-inch
    seam. Flip the lace over to the right side of the stocking and press it down with
    an iron. You should have two stocking forms with the lace trim on the "right
    side" of the material.

3. Pin the two stocking forms with the right sides together. Sew around the sides
    and bottom of the stockings using a ½-inch seam. Cut slits into the bias of the
    seam around the corners to prevent the material from puckering. Turn the
    stocking right-side-out and iron it flat.

4. Glue a piece of trim across the top of the stocking. Glue another piece of trim
    along the heel and toe area of the stocking. Form a loop and stitch a piece of the
    trim onto the upper-left corner for hanging purposes.

5. Write a name on the lace trim with the squeezable fabric paint. If desired, sew a
    gold bell onto the side of the stocking.

Here are some basic tips and techniques that can help take the hassle out of sewing fabric. First of all, be sure you have a flat working area to lay out your material. You should have special sharp scissors that you only use to cut fabric. Press your material before using it, and pin the area to be sewn together with straight pins to keep it from slipping apart when sewing it. Always leave at least a ½-inch margin around the edge of the seam and cut slits in this margin around the curves to keep the stitches from puckering. (Be careful not to cut the thread when doing this.)

Embellished Boxes

You can transform ordinary cardboard boxes into these lovely decorative boxes in no time. Use sturdier gift boxes from department stores, or buy relatively inexpensive cardboard boxes at a craft store for this project.

Using foil rub-on transfers to create a decorative box.

(Melissa LeBon)

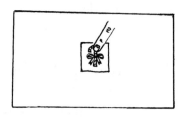

Level: Moderately easy

Time involved: Two hours, including drying time

Materials:

Cardboard box

White craft paint

Paintbrush

Foil rub-on transfers (You can buy these in kits at a craft store.)

Scissors

Clear acrylic finish spray

Decorative ribbon

Glue gun

Excelsior moss or crepe paper filler

1. Paint the outside of the box and the lid with white craft paint and allow it to dry.

2. Keeping the protective sheets of the transfers together, cut out your selected foil design. Peel off the protective paper sheet and press the design onto the lid of the box with your finger. (Do not rub the design.) Slowly peel off the protective plastic sheet.

3. Cut the foil the same size as your design. Place the foil over your design with the shiny side facing up. Carefully press the foil down onto the adhesive design and slowly peel off the foil sheet. Repeat this process on two opposite corners of the box lid. Spray the box with clear acrylic finish spray.

4. Glue a piece of decorative ribbon around the lid of the box. Make a small bow out of the ribbon and glue it in the center of the box lid. Fill the box with excelsior moss or crepe paper filler before adding your gift.

While you're working on this project, try this special treat to stimulate your creative juices: Make some hot cocoa and let it cool slightly. Break off the curved end of a candy cane and stick the straight end in your cup of cocoa to use as a straw. You'll love the minty taste the cocoa acquires as it flows through the candy-cane straw.

Guess What?

There are many legends surrounding the candy cane. One legend states that the candy cane was designed by an elderly man to display his love of Jesus. The candy cane is in the shape of a shepherd's staff which, when turned upside down, forms the letter "J" for "Jesus." The white stripes represent the virgin birth and the red stripes symbolize the blood that was shed by Jesus upon his death. The peppermint flavoring resembles hyssop, an herb from the mint family, which was used for purification and sacrifice.

Wrapping It Up in Style

Homemade wrapping paper is fun and easy to make. Get the kids involved and see how many different designs you can create.

Level: Easy

Time involved: Two to three hours, including drying time

Materials:

> Roll of white or brown craft paper
>
> Scissors
>
> Protective plastic or newspapers
>
> Craft paints
>
> Foam plate
>
> Paintbrushes
>
> Christmas stamps or sponges

1. Cut a piece of craft paper the size of your package. Lay the paper on a flat working surface protected by plastic or newspapers.
2. Pour a small amount of different colored paints onto the foam plate. Using a paintbrush, paint the stamps or sponges with the desired color. Stamp a pattern of Christmas designs across the paper. Allow the paint to dry before wrapping your gift.

Children's After-Christmas Crafts

Let Christmas vacation bring out the kid in you. Finish off a lovely day of sledding or skiing with a quiet craft session in front of the fireplace. Or if you live in a warmer climate, throw on a Christmas CD and enjoy the snow experience by making your own snow globes and snowflakes.

Let It Snow!

Why pay big bucks for a snow globe when you and your kids can design your own for pennies? It's simple to transform a plain glass jar into a winter wonderland scene created to your specifications. You might want to make several scenes, one for each of the bedrooms.

Level: Easy

Time involved: One to two hours

Materials:

> Old jars with lids (Mason jars, peanut butter jars, and baby-food jars work well.)
>
> Glue gun
>
> Plastic Christmas figures (Check craft or hobby stores for the figures used in "under-the-tree" scenes.)
>
> White rocks, marbles, or decorative glass pieces
>
> Water
>
> Food coloring (optional)
>
> White glitter and/or white confetti (Use metallic or plastic confetti, not paper.)

1. Wash and dry the jar and the lid. Glue the figures and the rocks to the inside of the jar lid using a glue gun.
2. Fill the jar with cold water to within ⅓ inch of the top. If desired, add a drop of food coloring (blue makes a nice sky effect). Add 2 tablespoons glitter and/or confetti.
3. Squeeze a line of hot glue around the inside rim of the lid. Immediately seal the jar with the lid.

You might want to try making paper snowflakes to go along with your snow globes. Start with a square piece of paper and fold it in half diagonally three times, keeping track of the center with your thumb. Cut half of a snowflake ray along each folded side of the paper, moving toward, but not cutting through, the center of the paper under your thumb. You should have a V-shape design with the bottom point of the V being the center of the paper. Cut more designs into the paper, making sure to leave some sections of the folded edges together so the snowflake will stay together when unfolded. Open your snowflake, and decorate it with glitter if desired.

Wired Wonders

Jewelry wire is a fun craft medium that you can shape into various designs. This wire is perfect for making unique photo frames or room decorations. You can follow the patterns detailed here, or try your hand at creating your own lovely designs. You might want to have a family contest to see who can come up with the most original creation.

Whimsical wired decorations.

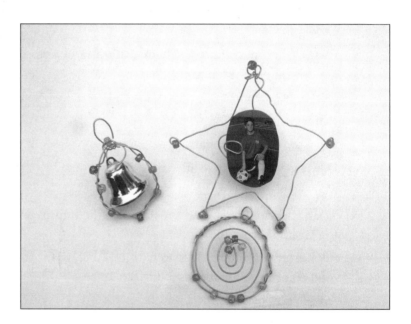

Level: Easy

Time involved: Half to one hour

Materials:

> Three different colors of 18-gauge jewelry wire (I used green, gold, and blue.)
>
> Tape measure
>
> Wire cutters
>
> Plastic *pony beads*
>
> Small photograph (for star ornament)
>
> Gold bell (for bell ornament)

Plain and Simple

Pony beads are round plastic beads that are sold in bags in craft stores. These beads come in assorted colors and can be used in many different craft projects. If your kids enjoy working with beads, I'd recommend buying a pony-bead project kit for a rainy day.

To make the star:

1. Using wire cutters, cut a 30-inch length of gold jewelry wire. Start at one end of the wire and form a 2-inch-long star point. Thread a red pony bead onto the end of the point and twist the wire around it to hold it in place. Form a second point, and twist a green bead onto the end. Continue to make points until there are five points forming a star, with pony beads on the end of each point.

2. Twist the remaining length of wire into a spiral, and center the spiral inside the star. Insert a small picture into the spiral shape.

To make the spiral decoration:

1. Cut an 18-inch piece of blue jewelry wire. Twist the wire into a spiral-shaped ball, creating a 3-D effect inside the ball.

2. Thread the pony beads onto alternating wire loops of the ball.

3. Cut a 10-inch piece of green wire and wrap it around the top of the ball, forming a small loop at the top for hanging purposes.

To make the bell hanger:

1. Cut a piece of green wire 15 inches long. Form the wire into an oval shape, leaving 3 inches of excess wire on either end at the top. Bend the excess wire on one end into a loop on top for hanging the ornament and the excess wire on the other end into a loop on the inside for hanging the bell.

2. Thread the gold bell onto the inside loop and twist the ends together at the top.

3. Cut a second piece of wire 12 inches long and, starting at the top of the ornament, twist the wire onto the first piece of wire. Add a pony bead and twist again. Add another pony bead about ½ inch away and twist again. Continue around the ornament until you reach the other end.

Christmas Cooking Crafts

Nothing is quite as special as a handcrafted gift that tastes great. You can make these goodies for the people on your gift list in no time and pass on or start a new family tradition from your kitchen.

Cookies to Go

The basic method to making cookies in a jar is to layer the dry ingredients into clean jars and pack them down. A recipe should be attached to the jar, describing how to assemble the remaining ingredients and bake a finished cookie. A decorated Mason jar works well with these delicious creations.

Making cookies to go.

(Melissa LeBon)

Level: Moderately easy

Time involved: One to two hours

Materials:

> Clean Mason jar with lid
>
> Piece of fabric
>
> Rubber band
>
> Ribbon
>
> Two cinnamon sticks
>
> Piece of holly
>
> Cookie recipe

Adhesive label

Paper

Fine-tip marker or computer

Hole punch

1. Choose a favorite cookie recipe or use the one that follows.

2. Combine the flour and baking powder and stir well. Pack the mixture in a clean Mason jar. Add the sugars and pack this down. Add oats, coconut, and cereal, or any other dry ingredients (such as chocolate chips, nuts, or raisins).

3. Put the lid on the jar and screw down tightly. Place a square of cotton material on top of the lid. Gather the material around the lid and secure it with a rubber band. Tie a ribbon around the mouth of the jar, forming the ends of the ribbon into a bow. Catch a couple cinnamon sticks and a sprig of holly in the bow.

4. Print the name of the cookie recipe on the label and stick it on the jar. Print the recipe on a piece of paper. (You could use a computer for this.) Fold the recipe in half and punch a hole in the top corner. Thread a piece of ribbon through the hole and attach the recipe to the ribbon on the jar.

Ranger Joe Cookies

½ cup butter or margarine	½ cup brown sugar
½ tsp. baking soda	½ cup granulated sugar
1 TB. cold coffee	1½ cups quick oats
1 large egg, beaten	½ cup flake coconut
1 cup flour	1 cup krispy rice or wheat cereal flakes
½ tsp. baking powder	

Preheat oven to 350°F. Cream butter or margarine until fluffy. Stir baking soda into cold coffee and set aside. Add the beaten egg to the mixture and blend well.

Stir in dry ingredients from the jar and add coffee mixture. Blend until well combined.

Roll dough into small balls and place on a greased cookie sheet 2 inches apart. Press the ball flat with a fork. Bake at 350°F for 12 to 15 minutes or until golden brown.

If you liked making the cookies in a jar for your family and friends, you might want to try putting the dry ingredients for brownies or other dessert bars in a jar. You could also provide the ingredients for cut-out cookies and include some cookie cutters and tubes of icing with the gift.

Cinnamon Cut-Outs

These cinnamon creations not only look nice, but they also smell great! Bring the heavenly aroma of baking cookies to your home by making these decorative cinnamon ornaments.

Level: Moderately easy

Time involved: Two to three hours, plus one to two days to dry

Ingredients:

> Mixing bowl
>
> Spoon
>
> 1 cup ground cinnamon
>
> ⅔ cup applesauce
>
> 1 TB. white glue
>
> Rolling pin
>
> Cookie cutters
>
> Cookie sheets
>
> Paintbrush or skewer
>
> Fabric paints in squeeze bottles

1. Mix cinnamon, applesauce, and glue in a bowl until they form stiff dough. If mixture is too thin, add cinnamon; if too dry, add applesauce.

2. Using a rolling pin, roll the dough out to about ¼ inch on a surface lightly sprinkled with cinnamon. Cut shapes out of the dough using Christmas cookie cutters. Place the cinnamon shapes on a cookie sheet and make a hole in the top using the sharp end of a paintbrush or a skewer. Allow the cut-outs to dry for 24 to 48 hours, or bake them in a 250°F oven until hard. You could also make these ornaments free-form by following the illustrations.

3. Decorate the ornaments with fabric paints in squeeze bottles.

Cinnamon cut-outs take time to dry. You can bake them in a 250°F oven to speed up the process, but be sure not to overbake them or to bake them at too high a temperature, or they will crack. Cut-outs take one to two days to air dry. You might want to sand any rough edges with a piece of fine-grain sandpaper before painting them. A layer of varnish will protect your creations over the years.

You can also make Christmas ornaments out of salt dough that puffs up when you bake it. Just mix 2 cups flour, 1 cup salt, and 1 cup water together in a bowl. Knead the ingredients with your hands until they are well blended. Roll the dough onto a lightly floured surface to a ¼-inch thickness and cut out shapes with cookie cutters. Make a hole in the top of the shapes for hanging purposes. Bake them in a 350°F oven for 8 to 15 minutes or until the dough turns golden brown on the edges. Allow the ornaments to cool and then paint them with craft paints. Spray the dry-painted ornaments with clear acrylic finish spray for a lasting finish.

Part 3

Parties and Get-Togethers

Creating, recording, and preserving family memories can be one of the most joyful of your parenting responsibilities. As you celebrate the important milestones in the lives of your family and friends, a little extra time and effort spent in planning can reap bountiful rewards in the precious memories these events create.

With careful planning, every party and get-together can be used to show honor and love for the person or event you are celebrating. Adults and children alike will appreciate the love and care given in planning a party that is unique and personal, as well as fun! Anniversary celebrations are a wonderful way to honor and validate the importance of God's gift of marriage. Housewarmings, graduation celebrations, and other acknowledgments of the good gifts from above will provide your family with warm and loving memories. And don't forget to record and preserve those memories—scrapbooking is just one of many ways you can provide a lasting record of the enduring bonds that your family shares.

Family Memories: Making Connections for Life

Memories are more than reminiscence of the past. Memories bridge our past and future and provide a moral compass for our present life. Our family memories are part of our spiritual heritage that we need to preserve and pass on to our children so that that they can someday pass them on to their children, and so on.

We cannot ignore the making of memories—we are making memories every day. Some stick and some don't and which is which is often a blessing from God. The question for your family is "Are we making good memories or bad memories?"

Simple Memories

Our family once saved for a long time to spend lots of money on a family vacation—Disneyland, Sea World, the beach, the works—and we bought a new camera and took rolls and rolls of photos to make sure we would remember every detail. Only, out of a dozen rolls of film, all but two rolls were completely destroyed at the end of the trip.

That's the Spirit

The ancient Israelites set up stones of remembrance to recall what God had done for them. "Each of you must pick up one stone and carry it on your shoulder—twelve stones in all, one for each of the twelve tribes. We will use these stones to build a memorial … They remind us that the Jordon River stopped flowing when the Ark of the Lord's covenant went across." (Joshua 4:4–7) What can you do to remember the Lord's work in your life?

From that experience, we coined a family phrase: "Make a memory!" Now when we recognize that we're participating in something we want to remember, we don't need film to record it. We tell each other to "Make a memory!" In short, we stop and focus our attention on what is happening—how we feel, what we see, the wonder of being together in that moment.

Big family vacations are fun and worthwhile. It would be tragic, however, to spend half a lifetime planning, working weekends, and eating mac-n-cheese only to spend a week or two with oversized cartoon characters in endless lines and crowds and never really make a memory worth keeping. Sometimes it happens—but it doesn't have to cost a lot of money.

My point? Live for the here and now, and make memories from the everyday. Some of the fondest memories come from evenings spent with friends, laughing over chips and dip and dominos; or Saturday morning trips to breakfast and the park; or living vicariously in an era gone by with grandparents or elderly neighbors; or hot cocoa by a fire after sledding. The day-to-day moments are the stuff of truly cherished memories.

Family Ties

Share the responsibility of making and recording family memories with everyone in the family. If you have a child who enjoys drawing or writing, ask him or her to record a family event. Get Dad to write a note or letter to commemorate a special occasion. Mom is often keeper of the family memories, but the more the job is shared, the richer the tapestry of your shared family memories will become.

Building Your Stories

I love to look at the many photos of ancestors, but not just my own. I have found boxes and whole scrapbooks full of photos at antique sales and flea markets. They are nameless strangers long gone and forgotten. The photos tell a story—one memory book I found had documented what I suspect was an annual hunting excursion. I guessed hunting because of the photos of game hanging around the campsite. I deduced annual because the photos seemed to progress in age and era. I purchased the book and eventually donated many of the photos to a small historical museum near a site that resembled the one in the pictures.

Family Ties

Make time as a family to reminisce about the past. Include Grandma and Grandpa on occasion to get a different perspective. It's always interesting to view the same event through the eyes of others.

Plain and Simple

Objects and things worth remembering and recording, such as a collection of anecdotes, accounts, or mementos, are considered **memorabilia**.

The photos were only things, but they were also literal views into someone else's family and life. Sadly, the only writing in the book was a few dates, and some of the photos had the stamp of the developer from San Antonio, Texas. I was left to wonder, did they live there or were they passing through and had only had the photos processed there? What story lay hidden in San Antonio?

The story undoubtedly would tell of fun and frolic, play and tradition. No doubt the old album served family and friends well in their lives. They could browse through the pages and return to a relaxed day of sunny adventure, even if the present might have been a rainy, stressful evening.

Family memories are more than boxes of photos and *memorabilia*. They are treasures beyond value—a heritage to preserve and protect. As you reflect on your family memories, what are you doing to record and preserve them?

Technology—the Value and the Danger

Humankind has recorded memorable times since the beginning, with words and paintings on cave walls, on canvas, and in sketchbooks. I am so grateful for the inventions we have today that have enhanced this great tradition of recording memories. In particular, thank you, Lord, for the camera!

Now we can see and hear our memories through video and the ever-fluid technology of computers and digital recording devices. Who knows what will be next? Science fiction promises us holographic images. Whatever the means, the recording of memories lifts us up and blesses us and our children.

Don't be distracted by all the technology, though. How do I decide what technology should I go for, how much should I spend, how many days until what I know now is obsolete? Try not to miss the important moments in life by getting all caught up in the technological method. There are many ways to preserve family memories. Do what you love, and try always to remember simplicity.

Memories in Writing

The most fundamental (and perhaps most important) way to build memories is to write the stories down. When creating photo albums, invest the effort in writing down the memories that might seem so obvious to you. These will be precious prompts for you in years to come, and they will be all the more meaningful to family members. The photo album about the hunting trips had pictures, and to those who participated these images carried memories of great exploits. But to those of us who look on from a great distance, they are a mystery. Meaning is lost with the people who remain keepers of the memories.

Correspondence

Save cards, letters, notes, and postcards that recount even what might seem at the moment only to contain the most trivial details. I removed the hunting photos from the album I purchased and replaced them with postcards from the collection I had been building. Most of these antique postcards were also passed between people I'll never know or have any relationship with. But they carry little messages from one place to the next—tidbits about visits and birthdays, illness and health … nearly any subject you could imagine.

There was no room to pen a novel, so they are all short and to the very dear point. Their concentration and economy of words makes them all the more valuable. But short and concise need not be the only collectible. Letters are wonderful records of memories, and saving them may bless someone someday.

Childhood Writings

As a child I kept a periodic journal. I seemed to write mostly when I felt sad. When the sad spell was passed, I would often tear the pages out. I was embarrassed to have been so silly and determined to make my life forever different. I would be reformed.

My mother, who watched me struggle through my teen years, secretly retrieved the banished pages and saved them for me. When I got married, she gave me a box containing these and other discarded items from my childhood. As an adult, now, perhaps I can see a young girl from a grown-up's perspective and forgive her childish ways.

I've made it a point to keep notes from my children. I have tried to remember to add a date at least before tossing them into my "treasure" drawer. Every once in a while I will pull them out and read them—they are funny and heartwarming. Someday I will organize them and return them to the authors.

Document Your Children's Moments

When my first child was born, I received a baby book to record the milestones of my daughter's first year. I remember going over my own baby book with my mother—who recorded things like first smile, first word, first tooth—and important details like time of birth, birth weight, and length.

In my daughter's baby books, I have added all the normal stuff—dutifully filling in the blanks provided. But I have also included other important information. When I was pregnant with each of my girls, I prayed that God would give me a verse just for that child, and he did. Their verse is recorded in the front of their books along with a record of my thoughts just after their birth.

I tried to keep up both my daughter's baby books, though I wasn't nearly as thorough with the second one (perhaps because by the time she was born, I still had a two-year-old to deal with as well). Thank goodness their baby books came in a box so that during busy times, I could toss things that I wanted to add in the box to later be added to the book.

The boxes are starting to fall apart because the girls have gone through the contents so many times. But they still contain many precious memories and are a memorial to my daughters that they were loved from the time they were born.

Use Natural and Meaningful Methods for Recording

Another place to jot down special events, anecdotes, and other notables is right in the pages of a favorite cookbook. A double fudge cake recipe in my *Joy of Cooking* has a few entries by it. Even if a recipe fails me, I can record that entry, too.

More special yet can be a particular family Bible that serves not only to record vital family statistics (births and deaths), but that also contains Mom's and Dad's personal journaling of spiritual struggles and joys, placed in the context of passages that were relevant to his or her life at the moment. Not only will this be a cherished archive for generations to come, but it will also reveal your testimony to the relevance of God's Word in your own life.

Lives can be recorded on tape and CDs now. If you are more comfortable having conversations than writing, then this is a good direction for you to go. Audiotapes and videos have served us well, allowing faraway loved ones to participate in our lives. But beyond that, they also serve as precious records for decades to come of dear people and their stories—of their gestures, inflections, endearing quirks, and the life issues of the moment. Try not to relegate the video camera to merely special occasions. Get out the devices on ordinary days and start recording life for posterity.

Be Practical and Purposeful About Memory Making

The following are some suggestions for tools that can help you record your life memories:

- A Family Prayer Treasury. A compilation of sayings, blessings, praises, accounts, and Scripture references that have come to define your family as it grows.
- Notes in your Bible. Dedicated Scripture and comments from studies, including cross references given.
- Calendar notes. Don't be too quick to throw away last month's page.
- Cookbook notes.
- Journals from your children, even from children to parents.
- Letters from parents to children, to be read when children are older.

- Candlelit table talk. Take time to share and to sing, perhaps around the advent season, and again midyear to remember holiday spices and the joy the Christmas season so often brings.

- Send yourself a postcard from a vacation destination. (Note to self.) And hang on to those sent to you by others. Archive them as soon as you can, rather than stuffing them away in a drawer or shoe box.

- Keep a box or book of family recipes.

- Make a treasure box for each child, and save a few outfits, a favorite toy, some school work, letters, photos, etc.

- Have a Family Video Night, complete with popcorn and home movies. Have slides transferred to video or a CD to add Mom and Dad to the baby parade. View those old favorites with the kids, like "Our Wedding Day" and "The Day You Were Born."

- Give gifts with stories attached.

Gifts with stories behind them serve as tangible links to the past. Maybe there's your Grandmother's candy dish—the one she won at age 10 during a visit to the county fair. Why should this matter to you? Because she was once young, just as you were. She loved life and experienced its ups and downs, and without her there would be no you.

When my grandmother died, I was handed a shoe box with a baby doll in it. I already knew the story. My oldest brother eloped when he was 18 years old and I was 12. My grandmother wanted to host a small wedding reception for the young couple, and I was dispatched to her house to help set up. Always the party-organizer, Grandma needed a centerpiece for her buffet table that matched the theme of the occasion. So she sent Grandpa out to buy a doll dressed in a bridal dress. Poor Grandpa came back with a baby doll in a white gown and bonnet. He said he thought it was a bride. (I have to smile now just remembering the scene.)

That moment is one of my clearest memories of my grandparents, who have been gone now for many years, and that doll is now almost 40 years old. When I came home from my grandmother's funeral, I was able to share that story with my girls because of the memories that doll evoked. And someday one of them will have the doll and the memories.

Remembering Is Key

Memories are important to God, and they're important to us, too. Whenever in history there has been a question of God's love or God's faithfulness, he has always responded to his people by challenging them to remember how he has saved them, be it God's deliverance of Israel through the Red Sea or Jesus' last supper. That's because memories are fundamental to how we live our lives in the present.

Likewise, when we remember the people, joys, and sorrows of our past, we give meaning to our present. Memories cannot bring back the past, nor can they make people who have left us alive again (despite what so many modern philosophies and stories try to convince us). But they can root us in the present and even encourage us as we live on. And for us believers, memories first and foremost reinforce how God has been faithful to us, guiding us throughout our lives. This is why memories are important to invest in and preserve for ourselves and for generations to come.

That's the Spirit

Want to know the secret to creating good family memories? Choose to focus on the good things that are happening in our lives and the work God is doing in our families.

Fix your thoughts on what is true and honorable and right. Think about things that are pure and lovely and admirable. Think about things that are excellent and worthy of praise.

—Philemon 4:8

Chapter 18

The Theme Says It All

Get-togethers with family and friends—birthdays, anniversaries, a barbecue, or tea party—are cause for celebration, whatever the occasion or its style. And celebrations are the stuff that happy memories are made of. Now plan your get-together around a theme, and you can multiply the excitement and crank up the memory-meter. A theme adds a dimension to events that most gatherings lack. It brings up the level of interest and unites the guests before the party even begins.

In this chapter, you'll learn how to organize your get-togethers around a theme—adding party pizzazz to every occasion. You'll learn how to excite your guests with theme invitations, decorations, and even food. You'll also see how having a theme can make planning easier.

Is a Theme Necessary?

Is a theme necessary for you to host a successful celebration? Perhaps not. Desirable? Let's explore that. Here are two party examples—you choose the party you'd rather go to.

- **Party 1.** You go to your mailbox and find a store-bought party invitation. It's a standard greeting card with a balloon design imprinted on the front. You open it, and handwritten in the very small spaces provided, it says: "We're having a party!" It gives the names of the hosts, address, phone number, and date.

Handwritten on the back of the card (because there is no proper place provided to write it), it reads: "We want to show off the videos of our trip to China. Hope you can make it. Dress is casual. Buffet and cocktails will be served."

Ho-hum.

- **Party 2.** Your doorbell rings. When you open the door, your letter carrier hands you a cardboard mailer (a Chinese take-out box). The carton, trimmed with large Chinese lettering, has on it a shiny red label in the shape of a dragon that bears your name and address. You open it and there you find a fortune cookie, a tea bag, and a colorful paper fan along with an invitation printed on a post-card of the Great Wall of China. The invitation reads: "Join us for video high-lights of our journey to the mysterious Orient, along with cocktails and a *Szechwan, Mandarin,* and *Cantonese* buffet supper. We begin our journey down the Yangtzee River at 8 P.M. on Saturday, January 20, 2003. Call 989-555-2938 by January 10 to reserve your place in our pagoda. Mandarin garments encour-aged. Bill and Nancy Smith."

Plain and Simple

Many of the foods in **Mandarin** cuisine are wheat-based, instead of rice-based, con-sisting of dumplings, breads, and noodles. The food is mild in taste.

Cantonese food is the mildest and most common kind of Chinese food.

Szechwan food is liberal in the use of garlic, scallions, and chilies on chicken, pork, and seafood.

Now, which party would you rather attend?

The first example is the way we are usually invited to parties. It's functional … but boring. From the invitation, you know you will spend an evening watching home movies from your friends' recent trip. These occasions have a boredom stigma and are often successful as a cure for insomnia.

The second one immediately tells you this is going to be an interesting party. In fact, if the party lives up to the magic of the invitation, it's going to be unforgettable. This has to be more than a boring evening watching home movies. A party like this will not only be memorable, but possibly educational and definitely exciting.

That's the Spirit

A well-planned party doesn't have to be expensive or elaborate. The idea is to plan an occasion that honors others and shows love.

A bowl of soup with someone you love is better than steak with someone you hate.

—Proverbs 15:17

Now, isn't that the way you'd want your guests to look forward to all of your parties?

In the case of the second party, your friends have not only sent out a unique invitation, but have also chosen to wrap the entire party around a Chinese theme. It makes perfect sense. The films are of their trip to China, they probably have brought back interesting souvenirs, and it's an easy theme to carry through. Why not make the experience of watching the video as exciting for their friends as taking the trip was for them?

Sometimes choosing a theme is not as obvious, and you will be required to use a little creative imagination when coming up with your theme.

Let the Occasion Set the Theme

Chances are you have already held a number of parties with simple themes. Have you ever purchased birthday party goods imprinted with "Over the Hill," or a golf design, or scenes from a nursery rhyme? Those are themes.

You can make any holiday event extraordinary by expanding on a theme. For example, "Trim a Tree" is a very common theme for Christmas. However, you can make a simple holiday party unique by taking the typical holiday and adding a twist—"Stars and Stripes Triathlon." By giving a holiday another added dimension—like sports—you have made a holiday celebration more memorable.

Sometimes if you just move the routine date of an event, it's enough to create a festive atmosphere that brands it truly special. If you want, host a "Christmas in July" party, or in May have an "Every Night Is New Year's Eve" theme party for a person who adores the holiday season.

You see you don't have to create something new, you just have to move it out of context to make it reappear in an exciting way.

Kids' Play

Kids' parties are usually theme-related. In fact, there is a huge industry devoted to designing preprinted party goods of a favorite cartoon or comic character, sports, dolls, space travel, or other child-friendly subjects. It is so easy to buy these products. Just go into the store or an online vendor and pick out every item that's in a particular line.

The problem is that while such party goods are festive, they are also perhaps too familiar or common for some people.

Crafty parents will often produce extremely individualized themes for their children's parties by creating their own invitations, decorations, costumes, favors, and fun foods. When this is the case, the whole family often joins in to make a party of preparing for the party.

There is nothing wrong in buying prepackaged theme designs. They can be very helpful if you feel your skills are lacking or you're just short of time. However, with very little effort, you can still make these party packages more personal and unique.

Parties by Design

Why should the kids get to have all the fun? There's no reason that big kids can't hold a theme party with a little more adult pizzazz—not when there are so many ways of shaking things up and coming up with a fabulous bash. Shouldn't a sixtieth anniversary party, planned for a couple who were wed during the big-band era, swing? Or how about basing a graduation celebration for a finance student around the trappings of big business and Wall Street?

You can invent your theme by looking around your surroundings. This is particularly effective when you are starting out because it means you don't have to fight your décor—you work with it. It's very difficult to hold a *Lost in Space* party when you are surrounded by furniture that looks as if it belongs in a ranch house in Texas. You can do it, of course, but it takes a lot more work and money to transform it. Why fight it? Look at your furniture. Even if it's a mishmash, chances are there is at least one style that stands out. Let the design decide the feeling for the event, then all you have to do is create a theme to suit the occasion and the surroundings.

An eager hostess invited her guests to celebrate her new washing machine at an impromptu all-white dinner party. Within hours she had tumbled together a menu, table décor, and party favors for her "blanc" bash. Getting into the spirit, the guests dressed in white and brought small gifts like detergent, bleach, and softeners, for the new "occupant."

It's a Grand Old Flag

Is your décor Early American? You can plan a colonial party featuring Yankee pot roast and flags on display to honor Betsy Ross, the creator of the first American flag. Then hold a rousing sing-along of patriotic songs. If it's not a general celebration but a milestone birthday, give the theme a patriotic plug such as "He's a Grand Old Man."

Guess What?

In June 1776, Betsy Ross was a brave widow struggling to run her own upholstery business. Upholsterers in colonial America not only worked on furniture, but also did all manner of sewing work, which included making flags. According to accounts given by Betsy Ross, General Washington came to her home and showed her a rough design of the flag that included a six-point star. Betsy, a standout with the scissors, demonstrated how to cut a five-point star in a single snip. Impressed, George Washington entrusted Betsy with making our first flag.

Futuristic Festivities

Is your furniture style high-tech? If so, a futuristic celebration would be more appropriate. Show off all your technological devices and set them up against your chrome and glass furniture. You and your guests can play virtual or video games. Serve freeze-dried cuisine, like the meals eaten by astronauts, or have guests place their dinner orders online or via a fax. This atmosphere would be ideal for a graduation, retirement, engagement, or going-away party with the title, "Here's to Your Future." High-tech styles also work well with "Man of the New Millennium" or space theme parties.

Using Your Surroundings

Wicker and rattan furniture will set the scene for a luau, beach party, or some oriental themes.

def·i·ni·tion Plain and Simple

A **smorgasbord** is a Scandinavian buffet offering a variety of hot and cold foods.

Likewise, a Danish Modern setting calls for a *smorgasbord*, while an English Tudor is perfect for either a formal dinner with Beef Wellington or a meal in a lively pub complete with fish and chips and dart games.

If your home is made up of a wide variety of differing styles too numerous to define, then use this to your advantage. Create a "Pieces of My Life" party and tag each item that has a great story: "Found at Goodwill thrift shop for $5 a week after I left home" or "Picked out of my neighbor's garbage late one night." Neither you nor your guests will ever again look at your furnishings without smiling at the memories.

If you want to further narrow your eclectic surroundings, look around your home and see if there is one focal point that draws everyone's attention. Is your living room dominated by a grand piano? A musical or concert party is the perfect choice. Use sheet music, books, or musical instruments to accent this theme.

When there is an important event happening, does everyone come to your place to watch your large-screen TV? You can be the producer of a theme party around a televised event like the Academy Awards, the Grammys, or the Super Bowl. Let the focal point of your home be the kick-off point for a black-tie-and-gown awards soiree or a sports spuds-and-suds day.

As you can see, any type of surroundings or focal point can be made to work to your advantage and turned into a theme.

Home Is Where I Hang My Hat

If looking at the inside of your home doesn't inspire you, look outside.

Live in an apartment building? You can pretend it's a high-rise penthouse. Get a friend to act as a door attendant outside your building to greet and usher in your guests. Make it a very chic and avant-garde event set in New York's *SoHo*. Or pretend you live in the notorious Dakota apartments across the street from Central Park. Consider the possibilities. What other stories can that building tell? Uptown or downtown, this theme will give your parties a new lease.

> **Guess What?**
>
> **SoHo** is a New York City neighborhood named after its location, SOuth of HOuston Street. SoHo is famous for the old industrial buildings that grace its streets and for the shops, galleries, and artists who reside there.

Do you live out on the farm or in the country? You can have a party at your homestead that will allow for some real stretching out. Outdoor locations lend themselves to casual themes like:

- "Westward Ho" (urban cowboy, Tex-Mex, cattle drive, barbecue)
- "State Fair" (If your friends can fruits, raise animals, grow vegetables—any activities you'd find at a State Fair—show them off at this party.)

- "Take a Break by the Lake" (terrific for having everyone come over for a dip in your own private swimming hole)

Guests can enjoy everything from volleyball to horseback riding in wide-open spaces. If you are lucky enough to live in the country, let it be the scheme for your theme.

Love Will Keep Us Together

There is really no limit to taking a typical celebration and giving it some sizzle. When it comes to anniversary parties, there is a good plan for any year, from the first to the seventy-fifth. You might pick the couple's wedding song as the central theme or trace their life together via several song titles: "We've Only Just Begun," "She's Having My Baby," "Sunrise, Sunset," "Love Will Keep Us Together," and "I Would Still Choose You."

Here are some ways to choose your themes based on personal information about the happy couple:

- Select the ballads of a favorite singer of the celebrating couple, or pick the music of a particular era that is meaningful to your guests of honor. Romance, nostalgia, and sentiment can be created by playing "their song."
- Where did they meet? For a fiftieth anniversary couple, replicate their favorite restaurant and the meal they enjoyed on their first date. Print a menu from that year with authentic prices, charge the guests for their dinner, and present the cash to the couple for a special meal—at today's prices.

Couples about to be married or wed from a few years to several decades will be thrilled with such thoughtful celebrations and will cherish the memories through their lifetime together.

If you are throwing a party for someone, you most likely know them very well; however, if you don't, contact his or her family or best friends to ask them about the habits and haunts of the guest of honor to help you with your theme selection.

That's the Spirit

When you make out your guest list, don't invite only your "rich and famous" friends. Consider the less fortunate you know who would love some entertainment. In the story of a great feast, Jesus says that the master told his servant: "Go quickly into the streets and alleys of the city and invite the crippled, the lame, and the blind." (Luke 14:21) This list would be especially appropriate at the holidays, when loneliness strikes hardest.

Leisure Pursuits

Symbols of hobbies, pastimes, and talents are great bases for a theme party. Have you been collecting comic books for a lifetime? Then why not hold a superhero party? (You will be surprised at how many adult men will be attracted to this theme.) This is a party strong in primary colors and whimsy (see Chapter 19).

Your passion for gardening will bloom in a "Ladies for Lunch" garden party. Use homegrown flowers, plants, and produce.

Is he hot-wired to ESPN's all-sports coverage? Then a gridiron idea is the perfect party plan.

Browse for Ideas

When you walk into your friend's home and it's filled floor to ceiling with books, you've got your theme right there. If novels are to his liking, scan his bookshelves for likely inspiration.

Family Ties

Should we admit it? Kids make great spies! If you need to do some "research" on your host, consider sending in the mini-troopers. Their natural curiosity is a great cover for uncovering ideas for a party theme.

Mysteries, detective stories, biographies, photography—whatever you discover can be developed into a party theme. Go to secondhand stores or garage sales to buy copies of old books or other items that work with your theme. Use them as favors or decorations.

Check out counters and shelves for other clues, too. What do they collect? Antiques? Model cars? Coca Cola memorabilia? Is their music collection spectacular? If you discover a coffee bean grinder, guess what? The idea is to determine a pattern that can be developed into a party theme:

- *Gone with the Wind* fan? This theme begs for mint juleps, fresh flowers, fried chicken, and southern hospitality. Your guests will gather on the verandah and party as if there's no tomorrow.
- Got a friend who is star-struck by Starbucks? Set up a little coffee shop experience with different flavored brews, biscotti, and buns.

Getting the idea? The most important rule for deciding on a theme is to consider the guest of honor and his or her personality, interests, talents, pastimes, and goals. You'll find the ideal theme for celebrating a person, and there is no better honor.

Couch Potato Chips

Just like a book party, you can easily make the same plans for the couch potato and his favorite TV shows, or the film fan and her selection of video picks. Familiarize yourself with your friend's habits and hobbies for clues to the theme party that would be a good fit.

Pastime Parties

Virtually any hobby can be adapted to a theme party. Bugs, bats, or birds—whatever your friend's pastime pursuits, you can create a theme that showcases what he or she loves.

For people who love to travel or someone with strong ethnic ties, theme parties with an international flair are the ticket. However, to give a generic international subject a twist, you can combine themes to create other variations. For example, if you choose a gambling theme, add some international adventure by setting the casino in Monte Carlo.

- A beach party is invariably fun, but it takes on a down-under dimension when you "put another shrimp on the *barbie*" for an Australian soiree. G'day, mates!

def·i·ni·tion Plain and Simple

Barbie is the Australian term for barbecue.

- For an anniversary party, consider where the couple honeymooned. A little Italian bistro, a French café, or a Hawaiian luau—maybe you can recreate some of the ambiance of the place?

Pack your party plan and treat your guests to an imaginary trip. No matter what your destination, your guests will love you for going that extra mile.

Time Tunnel

If you are brainstorming ideas, don't forget to look back in time to celebrate past eras. There were cakewalks and ice cream socials at the turn of the twentieth century. The 1920s brought prohibition, flappers, and bathtub gin. The "B-Boys"—The Beach Boys and The Beatles—epitomize the styles of the 1960s. Take a trip down nostalgia lane. Each decade is a source of theme inspiration.

Alternately, you can zoom ahead into the space age and true-life space exploration. The wonders of God's universe are pretty incredible!

Make Mine with a Twist

Although not really themes, serving styles can be the basis of a party. Clam bakes, barbecues, tailgates, potlucks, fish fries, or fondue cooking are among the ways of serving that are quite social and theme inspiring.

Several strategies are also party basics that can be built on. These include scavenger hunts, progressive parties, ongoing parties (like dining or tasting clubs), surprise parties, and housewarming parties. Here, too, you can blend a personalized theme with the strategy for a super event.

Set the scavenger hunt into a Valentine theme where guests have to collect pairs of treasures or all things red on their list. Or put the fondue party in a Swiss setting for a tasty trip theme.

Get creative. Explore every avenue available to look for theme inspiration.

That's the Spirit

Two thoughts on planning the perfect party:

Being happy doesn't mean everything is perfect. It means you have decided to look beyond the imperfections.

—Unknown

If you wait for perfect conditions, you will never get anything done.

—Ecclesiastes 11:4

Follow Through in All You Do

Finally, if you're still stuck, you can find multiple resources and books for total party plans. For instance, if you're online, check out www.PartyPlansPlus.com for a wide range of events planned from the invitation to the souvenirs.

Don't overburden yourself by trying to pull off the perfect party. That's not your goal. Remember to focus on two things:

- Have fun with the planning and preparations as much as with the event.
- If your guests have a good time, your party is a success.

The key to a successful theme celebration is to follow through. Start with the invitation and make sure you follow the theme with your choices of décor, menu, entertainment, prizes, and souvenirs.

Chapter 19

From Tots to Teens: Total Party Plans

One of the most exciting things about being a kid is that you look forward to your birthdays. It's always a time of friends and family gathering to celebrate. There is the fun of playing games and being entertained as the center of attention. Even though that might feel a little awkward, it is still, in the long run, an enjoyable experience for most.

So the next time you want to plan a big birthday blowout for your best buddy, your child, or a sibling, here are some ideas that will help you to make them memorable.

Classic Capers

It's a snap to plan theme parties for kids three to seven years of age. They are learning and discovering so much that they're interested in just about anything. And they don't have to work very hard at having fun. Many kids today enjoy some of the classic party themes you may remember from your own childhood—circus or carnival, pirates, jungle animals, and of course, cowboys.

Circus, Circus

What kid doesn't love the circus? It has everything children love—clowns, acrobats, animals, and junk food. Circus parties are as much fun to plan as they are to attend, and everyone in the family will want to join in.

Let Animals Lead the Way

Why not give out a box of animal crackers to your invited guests? Attach a note that gives the where, when, and why of the party, and you have a sweet treat of an invitation.

The Big Top

Decorating can be done with crepe paper streamers in bright colors. Pick a central spot on the ceiling in the party room (if there happens to be a light fixture there, all the better) and drape streamers from that point out to the corners and sides of the room to create a tent effect. Add some balloons and you've got a great circus atmosphere.

Three-Ring Entertainment

Consider setting up three separate activities that the children can rotate between on a given signal. Or do the activities together as one group. One activity might be outdoors or in an open room where they can practice tumbling, balancing, and other acrobatic-type tricks. Another activity could be putting the nose on the clown (a thematic version of Pin the Tail on the Donkey). Draw a clown face minus the nose on a poster board and attach to a wall or tree. Give kids cut-out red circles to try to stick on the clown's face in the right spot (blindfolded, of course).

Animal charades is more fun if it involves popping a balloon, too. Before the party, write the names of circus and zoo animals (lions, monkeys, bears, horses, etc.) on small slips of paper, stick them inside a balloon, and inflate and tie. For this activity, kids pick a balloon, pop it by sitting on it, read the animal name, and act out the animal for the others to guess. For nonreaders, use animal stickers or have someone whisper to them their animal. This is one to get on video!

Carnival Treats

Okay, no getting around it—this is a junk-food occasion. Corn dogs, french fries, and peanuts or popcorn are to be expected. You could also throw in some apple slices with caramel/peanut butter dip. For dessert, how about ice-cream cones or sundaes?

The Prize Sack

Take-home party bags can be simple white lunch bags that have been decorated with the circus theme. Add some candy and small animals and toy games—maybe include a helium balloon to take home—and your guest's circus visit is complete.

The Wild, Wild West Party

Children love to imagine being cowboys, and there are still plenty of books and movies out there to keep their interest in the West alive and kickin'. Most party goods stores will carry some supplies that will fit with a Wild West theme. If not, the traditional red-and-white checkered look works. Also, much of the mood can be created by everyone in the family dressing up in Western gear.

Gettin' the Word Out

Let your guests know they are wanted with a WANTED poster invitation. These are simple to draw up by hand or on the computer and reproduce with all the party details. The guest of honor can be Sheriff for the day with all the guests as honorary deputies.

Vittles and Fixin's

When it's time for the chuck wagon to roll into town, keep it simple. Serve a lunch of hotdogs and chips (baked beans and carrot sticks can also be added) in throw-away pie tins. You can have cowpoke punch (fruit punch) or root beer and a large sugar cookie or the traditional birthday cake.

def·i·ni·tion **Plain and Simple**

A **Western hoe-down** is like a square dance. Call out simple steps like circle to the left or right, skip into the circle, skip out of the circle, swing your partner, and promenade (couples walk hand in hand around the circle). You can also call for cowgirls to curtsy and cowboys to bow.

Rootin' Tootin' Games

Activities can take on a rodeo-type theme—roping a stump, galloping horses relay, Western duds relay (putting on boots, belt, and a hat and racing to the finish line). You might even try a *Western hoe-down* with simple steps. To slow things down, read a cowboy story or watch a Western.

The Cowboy's Reward

Party bags can be candy (stick candy adds an authentic touch) and a few small toys in a red bandana tied up with twine. You don't need to wait until sunset to send your cowpokes off to their own ranches. Parties for preschool children should be kept to about an hour; two hours is plenty for kids six to eight years old.

Speaking of Sports

Football, basketball, golf, horseback riding, gymnastics, soccer, baseball—whatever the interest of your guest of honor, he or she will have a ball at this party. You can focus on one sport, several, or all.

Invite guest athletes to try out for their spot on this all-star team. Suggest they come wearing team jerseys or T-shirts to support their favorite team. Whatever you do, here's an invitation idea to ensure that your guests have their ticket. Create a ticket for the big game that lists the party information to give your guests admission to the celebration using a desktop publishing program or clip art.

A party ticket to ride.

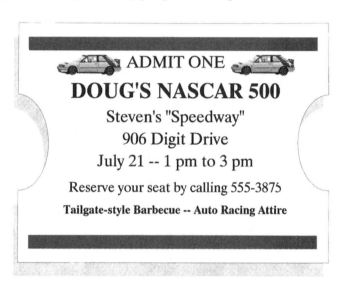

ADMIT ONE

DOUG'S NASCAR 500

Steven's "Speedway"
906 Digit Drive
July 21 -- 1 pm to 3 pm

Reserve your seat by calling 555-3875

Tailgate-style Barbecue -- Auto Racing Attire

Concession Stand

No day at the ballpark or stadium would be complete without a trip to the concession stand or buying a hot dog from one of the stadium's barkers. "Get ya red-hot hot dogs right heah!!"

![Family Ties icon] **Family Ties**

Serve food in cardboard trays, bags, and boxes to duplicate game-style gourmet.

Put together a menu of Ballpark Franks, pretzels, popcorn, peanuts in the shell, mini-pizzas, cotton candy, or whatever food is a favorite.

Have your server (could be Dad) wear the hat and apron of the ballpark hawker and carry the food in a tray he wears around his neck.

Are You Game?

If possible, organize everyone together in a short game of whatever sport you're focusing on. Many sports also have indoor or video versions.

If you have wide-open spaces and lots of folks, you might want to construct a field of play where guests go from game to game, or put together your own triathlon with running, jumping, and swimming (or whatever combination of activities you choose). Or watch filmed highlights or bloopers available at most video stores.

Furnishing the Field

Depending on the sport, you can give your "field of play" a variety of looks. For tennis, for instance, drape a long banquet table in green cloth or felt. Use white tape to create a tennis court and open-weave fabric to create the net. A similar approach would let you create a baseball diamond or a football field.

> **Guess What?**
>
> According to the U.S. Lawn Tennis Association, a regulation tennis ball, when dropped from a height of 100 inches on 4-inch-thick concrete, should bounce between 53 and 58 inches.

Whatever the theme, transform each table into something that suits the occasion. You can cover the table or just make a centerpiece to represent the sport. Party goods come in styles to represent almost every athletic pursuit.

Trophy Case

So that every guest goes home feeling like a winner, give blue ribbons, trophies, gym bags, or sporting equipment.

Entertainers Eatery

To emulate a filming atmosphere, set up *craft services* to offer continuous refreshments to the cast and crew. The type of menu you choose, to be laid out on long banquet-style tables, can take several directions. You might want to do a "build a better burger" bar, serve favorite foods of pop stars or stick to the choices of your guest of honor.

> **def·i·ni·tion** **Plain and Simple**
>
> The services provided by caterers on film sets are called **craft services**. The term is used for food-and-beverage providers for fashion shoots and film and video productions.

Soft drinks and water in sports bottles are a must, but if you want to toast the guest of honor, put nonalcoholic sparkling cider on ice.

Decorate the birthday cake to look like a stack of CDs. Talk about "cutting a record"!

A music audition invitation.

CASTING CALL

Do You Have What it Takes to be a Rock Star?

You sing the hits and we'll record your "audition" and you get to keep the tape.

You bring your own music or choose from one of our pre-recorded selection.

**Stacy's Sweet Sixteen
September 6
8 PM to Midnight**

473 Ises Road, Hartman

Please call to confirm your "audition."

(888) 555-1823

Quiet on the Set!

The entertainment at this party will be putting together video performances of the guest of honor and friends. They can choose to sing to backup music only, sing along with the recording star, or lip-synch completely. (Hey, karaoke is all the craze!)

A *karaoke* machine is a big help in putting together this entertainment. These are becoming more popular and less expensive, so if you don't have one, ask around and you will probably find someone who does. You also can download songs on the Internet. Otherwise, contact a local DJ service—some of them will bring all the needed equipment with them. You can focus on contemporary music that glorifies God (at least indirectly) by acquiring CDs of the latest Christian pop and rock stars. Just ask your kids, they'll probably be familiar with at least a few.

If you can't afford to hire a company, you can achieve a similar filming effect yourself. While it will likely lack professional quality, you can more than make up for it by using your imagination. Use your camcorder to shoot a variety of backgrounds like a forest, ocean waves, or even just the kitchen, and project them on a large-screen TV while your "star" is recording his or her tune.

Plain and Simple

Karaoke means "empty orchestra" and is a wildly popular entertainment concept that originated in Asia. The guests sing to the recorded background music, reading the words scrolling across a video screen.

If the guests are old enough, let them make the videos themselves. In fact, if you can arrange to get several cameras, you could have a couple of "film crews" working at the same time. Then you can act as the executive producer for all the projects.

Use a white board, chalkboard, poster board, or computer program to add titles and credit lines to the videos.

That's the Spirit

We were filled with laughter, and we sang for joy. And the other nations said, "What amazing things the Lord has done for them." Yes, the Lord has done amazing things for us! What joy!

—Psalm 126:2–3

The world's perception is that Christians don't know how to have fun. Non-Christians need to see the joy and laughter of Christian families who do not compromise their principles and who act as a testimony to God's goodness.

For fun that will last, set up a website where the videos can be uploaded. Because you never know who is checking the site, you might find one of your guests has been discovered. However, be sure to get permission from the participants and their parents before doing it.

Dressing the Set

Greet your rising stars with sound effects like screaming fans and sights of popping camera flash bulbs. Get older or younger siblings and their friends to play these parts.

Hang inflatable musical instruments, a shimmer curtain, giant records, and miscellaneous electronic equipment and other props around the "studio" for effect.

Great props for use in the videos can be found at garage sales, in attics, in thrift shops, and at swap meets.

That's the Spirit

Parties can occasionally be an excuse for bad behavior. Attitudes and words should be in the spirit of Ephesians 5:4: "Obscene stories, foolish talk, and course jokes—these are not for you. Instead, let there be thankfulness to God."

If you have pre-teens or teens in your home, planning fun parties for them and their friends that do not compromise your values is important. Encourage your kids to share the responsibility of keeping the festivities under control according to "house rules" you have established and discussed beforehand.

It's a Wrap

Each guest should receive a copy of his or her own performance, of course. However, it would be nice if everyone could also receive a copy of the other guests' performances. This would likely have to be sent to them at a later date to allow time for duplication.

Chapter
20

Congratulations Goes To ...

Life's most important occasions are those that mark a milestone such as a thirtieth, fortieth, fiftieth, or sixtieth birthday, or an anniversary celebration. Children grow from year to year celebrating not only birthdays, but also receiving degrees starting at kindergarten and advancing as far as earning the title of doctor in their chosen field.

In this chapter, you'll learn how to celebrate all of life's greatest milestones, from anniversaries to graduations. Remember, when it comes to parties, these celebrations are important and should be planned with the greatest care and love.

Love Is Still in Fashion

This anniversary party is a tribute to married love that, unlike fashion, has not faded through the years. This spoofs on "ages ago" apparel and accoutrements such as the Nehru jacket, leisure suit, or slinky polyester flare-leg jumpsuit.

There will be giggles and guffaws when your guests receive an invitation explaining the gist of the celebration. Their mental wheels will start turning with illusions of how garish or gaudy their outfits will be. Add the addresses and phone numbers of thrift and resale shops on costume party invitations.

It'll be a groovy invite, baby!

A truly "un"-fashionable invitation.

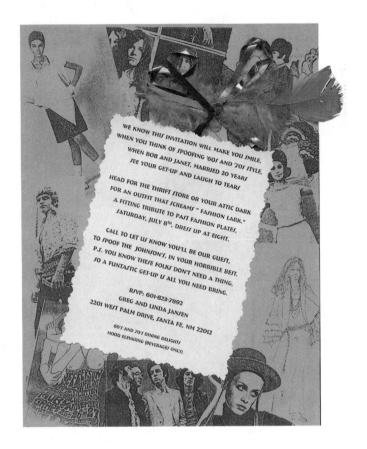

WE KNOW THIS INVITATION WILL MAKE YOU SMILE,
WHEN YOU THINK OF SPOOFING '60S AND '70S STYLE,
WHEN BOB AND JANET, MARRIED 20 YEARS
SEE YOUR GET-UP AND LAUGH TO TEARS

HEAD FOR THE THRIFT STORE OR YOUR ATTIC DARK
FOR AN OUTFIT THAT SCREAMS "FASHION LARK."
A FITTING TRIBUTE TO PAST FASHION PLATES,
SATURDAY, JULY 8TH, DRESS UP AT EIGHT.

CALL TO LET US KNOW YOU'LL BE OUR GUEST,
TO SPOOF THE JOHNSON'S, IN YOUR HORRIBLE BEST.
P.S. YOU KNOW THESE FOLKS DON'T NEED A THING,
SO A FUNTASTIC GET-UP IS ALL YOU NEED BRING.

RSVP: 601-823-7892
GREG AND LINDA JANSEN
2201 WEST PALM DRIVE, SANTA FE, NM 22012

60'S AND 70'S DINING DELIGHTS
MOOD ELEVATING (BEVERAGES ONLY)

Fad-Tastic Food

Lay out a spread for your hungry "has-beens" including snacks reminiscent of the 1950s, 1960s, and 1970s (or whatever was popular during the years you're highlighting): potato chips and onion dip, vegetables and dip, Hi Ho Crackers, Chex party mix, little pigs in the blanket, English muffin pizzas, Sloppy Joe's, and Swedish meatballs.

For decadent desserts, dish out brownies, Toll House cookies, s'mores, Rice Krispies treats, root-beer floats, hot fudge sundaes, and Coca-Cola in a bottle.

Far-Out Funtime for Fashion Flops

While the sights alone should keep the gang occupied for a good long time, entertain them further by comparing stories about "when we wore this" and "did you really wear that?" or "I mean, what were we thinking?"

Get hairy with Beatle bangs, Farrah flips, or *Mod Squad* Afros. Don't forget the tie-dye shirts, peace symbols, bell bottoms, and regulation army gear.

Let the guests of honor judge a funny and funky fashions show and award a "Best of the Worst" contest. Have one of your gregarious guests do the commentary and don't forget to get it on videotape!

Whether in platform shoes or go-go boots, your guests will want to get down and bop or boogaloo. Play the music of whoever rocked your world and have them dancing in the streets.

Take a serious, sweet moment and honor the anniversary couple with a reverent anniversary waltz or the song they used for the first dance at their wedding.

Decoration or Disaster

The fashion fads of the decades will dictate your party decorations and props. Forgotten fabrics and trims such as *tie-dye*, geometric, floral prints, neon colors, and florescents bring back the flourish of the 1960s and 1970s.

Hang both grungy and glamorous garments and accessories like hats, scarves, jewelry, and purses on the walls and stair rails. Drape them dramatically over furniture or from the ceiling. If you're going for a festive and fad-fashioned look, mix in tie-dyed balloons and streamers.

Light the site with a black light, lava lamps, and the ever-popular *pole lamp*. Deck the dance floor with a mirrored disco ball and don't forget to have a spotlight dance.

Don't forget the velvet paintings of doe-eyed children or Emmett Kelly–like clowns. Plaster the walls with posters of concerts, movies, or sports events. Hang a few plants from macramé holders and decorate doorways with beaded curtains.

> **def·i·ni·tion** **Plain and Simple**
>
> **Tie-dye** is a method of producing irregularly colored fabrics by tying the fabric with string before placing it in the dye.

> **def·i·ni·tion** **Plain and Simple**
>
> **Pole lamps** were popular in the 1950s and 1960s. They consisted of a pole that extended from the ceiling to the floor with three or more lamps on it that could be adjusted to shine in different directions.

Fashion Favors and Stylish Souvenirs

These retro items are fab as favors and prizes for your groovy guests: tie-dye ties, love beads, or oldies tapes.

"G" Is for Graduation

One of the easiest ways to establish a theme is to build your entire party around the first letter of the key word. A graduation party is ideal for this initial concept, especially if student earned lettered degrees like B.A., M.A., or Ph.D. So now, when this great goal has been reached, it is time to spell "party" with a G.

Obviously, the first thing to do is explain the gist of your G gimmick and all of the guidelines for the gathering. The invitation you send will be clear as glass and with a grade A message. Whether you decide to be grand or generic, use gilded or gold lettering, on gift wrap or a garbage bag, be sure to go for the gusto.

> **That's the Spirit**
>
> A blessing for the graduate: "May [God] grant your heart's desire and fulfill all your plans. May we shout for joy when we hear of your victory, flying banners to honor our God. May the Lord answer all your prayers." (Psalm 20:4–5)

Print the wording on a piece of 8½ × 11-inch goldenrod colored paper. Trim the edges with a fancy-edged scissors and run a metallic gold pen over the edges to create a gilded effect. Punch two holes 2 inches apart at the top center of the sheet, run an 8-inch length of gold ribbon through the holes and tie it into a bow. Mail in a 6 × 9-inch white envelope, addressed in gold ink, decorated with rubber stamp art or gold glitter. When you write "G is for Graduation" in big letters across the top side of the envelope, they will get the message.

Go for the Getups

Once the invitations have landed, your guests will be giving some thought to what they will bring as a G-rated gift. Some of the more gutsy guys and gals will even go all out and dress in G garb. Have a list of gifts and costume ideas handy. Guests can gussy up in gauzy gowns, groom's garments, gabardine, or gold lamé. Generous guests will give good or goofy gifts such as garters or galoshes. And won't the grad be grateful?

Goodies Galore

Go all out for this gastronomical gourmet; grilled or griddled food will be great. Along with a basic party menu of your choice, add the G-factor with a selection of snack items such as goose liver, Gorgonzola cheese, goat cheese, guacamole, Gruyère cheese, garlic bread, goldfish crackers, gefilte fish, Gouda cheese, gherkins, or grapes.

Desserts including glazed donuts, gingerbread, gingersnaps, guava, ganache, graham crackers, Granny Smith apples, gumdrops, and glorified rice will bring grins. Guide your guests through the grub line with small signs labeling the G-rations.

Graduation invitation.

"G" is for graduation, and we're glad to say,
John made the grade, it's a G-Letter day.
We're going to gather, to salute the guy,
Then he'll go to college, we'll say goodbye.

Bring the whole gang over, in casual gear.
We'll giggle and gab, and grab a beer.
The gimmick is the letter "G."
It's the gist of the whole party

At the Johnson's, June 15th, 4-9 PM
Please R.S.V.P. by June 10th 614-555-2823
(Gag Gifts only-Goofy or Gaudy)
Good Grub, too!

Graduation Glorifications

From the gravel drive to your garage, through the house and out to the gazebo, glorify every G as you go. You could even make up signs that label each of these items with a big G. When decorating, use every shade of the color green, from green goblets to a gallon jug. Drape the walls with gossamer and gauze, or suspend grapevine from the ceilings.

Gone with the Wind

Plan a full gamut of games for the guests, including gin rummy, a game of touch football on the gridiron, or mini-golf. They'll go gaga over scenes from *Grease* or *Gone with the Wind* flickering on the video screen, or the recorded sounds of George Gershwin, Glenn Gould, the Go-Gos, or Gale Garnet—all gems of gold-record fame.

Toast the glittering grad with a gang of "great going"s, "go get 'em"s, and glad-handings in a glorifying gala toast.

After the gaiety and giddyness subside and the graduate has said his good-byes to the guests, you can be guaranteed that your "G-whiz" get-together was great.

Guess What?

A legendary toast: In the Middle Ages, a piece of spiced toast was often added to a drink for flavor. In the seventeenth century, the story goes that in Bath, England, a man took a glass of the public bath water his fair maiden was in, put a customary piece of toast in it, and drank to her health. He then offered the glass to his friend, who declined the drink but said he would like the toast.

Go-Home Gifts and Gee Gaws

After Grandma and Grandpa have gloated over their grand-graduate's glory, it's time to send guests home with goldfish, gadgets, or games.

House Sweet House

What a thrill it is to buy a new house, especially a first one. Whether it's a bungalow for two or a condominium on the Cape, excitement and pride are abundant. It's an ideal time to plan a "come see the new house" party.

This theme is quite easy to produce and will be the ideal way to show a newly built house, a remodeled house, or a home with remodeling potential. Building and decorating materials such as fabrics, wallpaper, carpet, and tile samples, fixtures, general construction equipment, and building materials will be the frame of the plan.

Here's a definite "key" to a successful housewarming/open house invitation. Send either new or used metal keys that have been sprayed gold and affixed to a sheet on which the party details have been printed. The invitation begins, "Our new home is always open to you."

A key to your home.

THE DOOR

**TO OUR NEW HOME
IS ALWAYS OPEN TO YOU**

**Please come and take a
tour of our new home,
(now that's remodeled.)
We can't wait for you to see
what has kept us busy
every spare moment
for the last year.**

Open House: June 15, 2001, 2-6 PM

2546 Ivy Lane, Brighton, CA 98002

RSVP: (Yes or No, Please) 201- 568-0431

Your presence is our gift of choice.

Casual Attire   Light Refreshments

Because this is the first time most guests will have been there, include clear directions or a map. Also be sure to festively decorate your home with balloons or a banner, so guests can be certain they have arrived at the right home.

That's the Spirit

It's good to remember that while a new house is a blessing, it is not wood, bricks, or mortar that make a home. It is the love of the people who live there and their commit-ment to the Lord that are the real cause for celebration.

Lord, through all the generations, you have been our home!

—(Psalm 90:1)

Glad to Meet Ya!

Hang out the welcome sign, lay down the welcome mat, and put a light in the window. From the moment your guests step across your threshold, grace and hospitality are your hosting goals.

It's a particularly good idea to invite your neighbors to this open house. It's a great way to introduce yourself to them, and you will surely win them over.

Guess What?

A younger couple moved into a quiet neighborhood composed mostly of older retirees, and there was a little concern about whether they would fit in with the quiet residents. The couple posted a notice on the communal mailbox inviting the neighbors to their open house. Seventy-five percent of them attended, and many were thrilled to see their neighbors socially for the first time in years.

Decorative Dining

You may be hesitant to serve food in your new home. While understandable, it wouldn't be very hospitable not to. To increase the chances of your home coming out unscathed, select menu choices made up of bite-size pieces that don't require anything more than a toothpick and a napkin.

At open-house occasions, because guests might just pop in, serving light refreshments is the best option. Don't try to restrict your guests! That is, don't crowd them into your dining room or any other space too small to accommodate easy help-yourself food service. Leave that area for show, and set up a makeshift feeding station in a locale that has room to move comfortably.

Display and serve food in containers related to home improvement projects. Cover tables in dropcloths, blueprints, or fabric swatches. Use tile samples as hot plates. Arrange hors d'oeuvres in a new paint tray. Put utensils and napkins in a new paint bucket.

Washington Did Not Sleep Here

At parties like this, you don't really need a lot of activities; holding a tour, telling the story of how it all came to be, and visiting will provide the entertainment.

Open houses are ideal situations to use name tags. Make yours from paint sample chips.

Play background music. You can choose light classical music or the music of—sorry, have to say it—the Carpenters.

Don't Gild the Lily

If your home is newly built or remodeled, it is likely you will want your décor to stand out unobstructed. The addition of fresh flowers and low lighting (if in the evening) will be appropriate and provide ample ambience. Candles at night, if not in a position to get jostled, also would add an intimate tone to your housewarming.

> **Family Ties**
> Give children smooth wood scraps to use as blocks, or pieces of fabric or paint swatches to make art projects with for their home or yours.

Christian art is improving in sophistication these days. Scripture or prayers tastefully displayed is a covert witness to your neighbors as to your beliefs and may provide an opening to share the Gospel.

Make posters of "before" photos and try to display them from the same angle they were shot for a "before and after" look.

Basically, incorporate your decorating tools (paint, swatches, samples, tiles) into your table design.

Classy Keepsakes

Besides your warmth, send guests away with a home-decorating magazine, printed address labels, or a potted plant.

Warm your new home with the love of family and friends, and you'll live there happily ever after.

Chapter 21

Preserving Memories

Many people assemble "memory books" to help them record their personal or family history. These scrapbooks may include photos, letters and notes, ticket stubs, pressed flowers, awards and certificates, and all other kinds of memorabilia. Although scrapbooking seems to be a fairly recent phenomenon, scrapbooks have been around for many years.

Scrapbooking is still a wonderful way to preserve family memories, and it has become an activity that every family member can participate in—regardless of age or skill level. There are loads of Internet sites, classes, and professionals to help you get started.

This chapter shows what you absolutely must have to start a beautiful scrapbook and the scrapbooking terms with which you should be familiar. If you have an unlimited budget, you can go to the store and buy whatever you like without regard to cost. But if you're like me, you need to be careful with your money. So becoming familiar with the materials here will help you choose your purchases wisely.

Scrapbookese: Terms Every Beginner Should Know

If you were to spend an afternoon with fly-fishing fanatics, you would most likely miss much of their conversation. Like many other hobbyists, scrapbookers have their own lingo. The first time I walked into a scrapbook store, I heard so many new terms that I was lost in five minutes. To help you seem like a pro before you have even mounted your first photo, here is a compilation of basic scrapbooking terms you need to know before you go shopping.

- **Acid.** A chemically reactive substance often found in paper that fades photographs. Products that are acid-free help you preserve your photos and other paper mementos.
- **pH level.** This tells how acidic or basic something is. For scrapbooking, you want to use products that are low in acid and have a pH level of seven or above.
- **PVC (polyvinyl chloride).** This is harmful to photographs. You should use products that are composed of polypropylene in your scrapbooks.
- **Polyethylene** and **polyester.** Stable plastics that are safe for photos. Look for these names on labels of products you purchase for scrapbooks.
- **Lignin.** A naturally occurring substance in wood that can break down into acids over time. Lignin must be removed from the paper to make it last. An example of what lignin does is the yellowing of newspaper. Newspaper is low-quality paper that contains high levels of acid, as well as lignin. If you leave newspaper exposed to the sun for a few days, you can see how lignin breaks down into acids because it discolors and becomes brittle.

> **That's the Spirit**
>
> A family is literally a "museum of memories" to those who have been blessed with children.
> —James Dobson
> Children are a gift from the Lord; they are a reward from him.
> —Psalm 127:3

- **Acid-migration.** When an item that is acidic comes in contact with another item that is less acidic, the acid can transfer over. This happens when acid from paper, dirty skin, or any item comes in contact with other items, and the acid transfers over.

  You can't always tell if paper is acid-free by the label, so ask a store clerk for information. Many scrapbooking stores have policies regarding acid-free paper and will go so far as to guarantee that all their paper is acid-free, lignin-free, and buffered. So go ahead and ask!

- **Buffered.** A term used to describe products that are capable of maintaining the basicity of a solution; in other words, use buffered paper to neutralize acids that migrate from a photo to paper.

- **Archival.** A designation for products and techniques that prevent photos and important documents from fading, deteriorating, and yellowing over time.
- **P.A.T. (Photo Activity Test).** A test created by the American National Standards Institute that determines whether a product will damage photos. If a product passes the P.A.T., it is considered archival and safe to use with photographs.

- **Reversible adhesives.** These adhesives can be unstuck. Reversible adhesives are desirable if you think you might ever want to move an item in your scrapbook to some other place.
- **CK OK.** Designation given by a company called Creative Keepsakes; CK OK is the scrapbooking industry's equivalent to the Good Housekeeping Seal of Approval.

Guess What?

> In order to clarify the scrapbooking industry's standard terminology, the CK OK team has written a book called *Saving Our Scrapbooks*, which has an industry-standard glossary.

Use a pH testing pen to test the acidic level of paper products. The pen mark changes colors depending on the level of acid present.

To make sure you feel completely confident in the company of hard-core scrapbookers, you're going to have to learn the following lingo. Do this and you'll really be able to "talk the talk."

- **Crop.** (1) To cut or trim a photo. (2) A gathering of scrapbookers working on album pages and sharing ideas with each other.
- **Workshop.** A class in scrapbooking usually held at a store and taught by an expert. Participants bring photos and pages to work on and get advice from the instructor.
- **Page exchanges.** These are fun activities in which participants are invited to create a page to share with up to 10 other scrapbookers. Sometimes a theme is given, such as a holiday like Halloween. Each participant at a page exchange brings enough copies of an original page to trade with the others and goes home with as many different pages as there are members, as well as the inspiration of their fellow scrapbookers.
- **Product swap.** If you've got duplicates of products, such as paper or stickers, or some tools that you don't use anymore, such as decorative scissors or paper edgers, gather them together and call some friends. Ask them to bring their unwanted scrapbooking items to trade. After it's done, you've got a clean closet and tons of new products—free!

Family Ties

Scrapbooking is a great intergenerational family activity. Get Grandma in on it! She might have the extra time to help sort photos and arrange pages, and would probably love to be a part of this family activity.

- **Scrapbooking club.** Any group of scrapbookers that meet regularly to encourage each other and compare books. Their main goal is to scrapbook together and share products.

Why not start a scrapbooking club? If you don't have a store nearby where you can take classes, and you know some people who like to scrap, start meeting together at home or at your local library, or rent a place to meet. Some scrapbooking groups charge monthly dues that are used to buy new products that everyone can use.

- **Layout.** Grouping of pages in a scrapbook that go together. Most often a layout means two pages that lay side by side with the same theme, such as "Jacob's gymnastics program."

Now that you know some of the technical terms and the jargon, you won't be confused when you go into a scrapbook store, open a scrapbooking magazine, or go to an online scrapbook chat room. Last of all is a list of scrapbooking terms that might mean different things to different people:

- **Mount.** To stick a photo onto another piece of paper.
- **Double mount.** To stick two pieces of paper together and adhere a photo to the top paper. This is similar to layered mattes in framing.

That's the Spirit

Keep a list of answered prayers in your scrapbook to remind yourself of God's faithfulness.

When they call on me, I will answer; I will be with them in trouble. I will rescue them and honor them.

—Psalm 91:15

- **Embellishment.** This catch-all phrase refers to stickers, die-cuts, and other extras that you add to a page.
- **Heading.** The title on a page.
- **Title page.** The page at the beginning of a scrapbook or section, such as "Smedley Family Reunion, July 1999" or "Kwaanza at Keisha's, December 1995."
- **Theme.** The overall focus of the scrapbook, such as a Family Vacations album.
- **Page.** The bare paper that is the foundation of the scrapbook decorated with photographs, embellishments, and journaling.

- **Memorabilia.** Items other than photographs that can be included in a scrapbook, such as documents, certificates, artwork, and souvenirs.

Several different weights of card stock are available. Go ahead and experiment with them to find what you like, but keep in mind that different weights don't make a practical difference.

People sometimes ask why we don't use lightweight paper in scrapbooks. After all, it would seem to cost less. Of course you can use it, and there are some companies that sell lightweight paper, but heavy paper holds up better, and it doesn't always cost more.

Don't Get Stuck—Choosing an Adhesive

I'm going to confess something here: I used rubber cement and scotch tape in the first scrapbook I made for my son! Of course, it was seven years ago, I was a first-time mother, and I had no clue about scrapbooking other than clip art and gluing pictures in. Years later and with much more scrapbook savvy, I know that rubber cement destroys photos, and I now use *adhesives* that are not only safe for photographs but also affordable and easy to use.

A variety of adhesives exists on the market, and as long as you use one designed for scrapbooking, your photos will be safe. Whether you choose to use glue, tape, or paste is a matter of preference, whatever you find easiest to use and easiest to find. Read on to find out what kinds of adhesives are available.

> **def·i·ni·tion** **Plain and Simple**
>
> An **adhesive** is any substance that is used to make items stick to each other—glue, paste, tape, reversible adhesives, and so on.

CK OK Guidelines for Adhesives
(for Adhering Paper and Colored Photos to Paper)

Acrylic base or starch base

Reversible

Free from odors, migratory substances, and chemical additives

White or colorless

Nontoxic

Neutral pH: 6.5 to 7.5

After the glue is set, it must not soften, run, transfer, or have odor after it is dry

Must not alter the color of paper, images, or photographs

Must not discolor over time

Must pass the P.A.T. (Photo Activity Test)

A variety of adhesives is available for safe use in scrapbooks.

Singin' the Glues

Glue is available in different styles: There are traditional glue sticks, liquid glue pens, and bottled liquid glue. Some of these are stronger than others, so try out a few and see what works best for you.

- Glue sticks have glue in a stick form. They are a little messy but are reasonably priced and readily available.
- If you will be gluing many small objects, a liquid glue pen is a good bet. This type of glue comes in a pen form, and glue is distributed depending on the amount of pressure you apply to the tip.

- Bottled liquid glue distributes glue from a narrow tip that makes it easy to use with small items, such as tiny punches, die cuts, and scraps.

- Some glue pens come in a two-way adhesive. This type of glue has a very strong bond when it is wet. If you apply it and let it dry before adhering, the bond becomes temporary, meaning you can remove your photos and embellishments if necessary.

More Sticky Stuff

Tape is my favorite adhesive to use in scrapbooks because it is neat and easy to use. A tape roller with its quick-dispensing capabilities and reversible adhesive is a great choice. You can buy refills for it, which also makes it cost-effective.

Double tape has adhesive on both sides. To use it, simply place the tape on your scrapbook page and stick the photo or embellishment to the other side. Double-stick tape is also available in rolls. Just peel it, tear it, and stick it! Nothing could be easier. Tape is great because it doesn't spill and won't dry out like glue. It is also reversible.

For precut adhesives, photo splits, sold by the box, are a good option. To use photo splits, simply pull out as many tabs as you need from the dispenser and apply them to your page. Peel off the top layer and apply your photo to the adhesive. That's it!

Guess What?

The Xyron machine is a popular, though relatively expensive, adhesive option. You run an item through two rollers in the machine, and the machine applies adhesive to one side. Without using heat or electricity, the Xyron can also laminate. You can even create your own stickers with a Xyron! If you plan to do a lot of scrapbooking, consider investing in one.

The "Write" Tools

Be sure to purchase a few writing, or journaling, tools, because journaling is what makes a cute scrapbook into a storybook. At the very least, you need to record the names and dates of the photo subjects.

A simple, black felt-tip pen is definitely the best for journaling on your pages. The best tool for writing on the back of photos is a wax or grease pencil, which can be wiped off with a soft cloth, or a special pen called the Pilot Photographic Marker, which is a fine-tip, black permanent pen for use in writing on the backs of photos.

**CK OK Guidelines for Ink
(in Pens and Markers)**

Light-fast/fade-resistant

Waterproof

Odorless when dry, no solvent smell left

High resistance to change, i.e., permanent

Quick-drying

Nonbleeding and nonmigrating quality

Nontoxic

Must pass the P.A.T. (Photo Activity Test) if used with photographs

A Little Protection

Unless you consider fingerprints an embellishment, you'll want to keep your pages in protective sleeves called *page protectors*. It is satisfying to finish an extra special page and place it in its protector, and page protectors are great because they're easy to move. You can purchase protectors in a couple forms, from full-page to protectors with sections for photos. These make organizing your photos easy—just slip in the photo, add a note, and you're done. Try giving these protectors to grandparents so they have a place to put all those darling photos you send them.

def·i·ni·tion Plain and Simple

Page protectors are a great way to display and protect your pages. These plastic sheets are available in top- or side-loading styles and come with holes that allow you to place them in a three-ring binder.

If you are unsure whether a protector is made with PVC, try the smell test—sniff the product. If it smells like a vinyl shower curtain, don't use it.

Protectors are marketed in two different types: clear or nonglare. The nonglare type has an almost mattelike finish that reduces the glare from the page. I like the look of the clear page protectors, but they do tend to show little nicks and fingerprints more than the nonglare type does. This is, of course, a matter of preference, as both are safe for your books. See which you like better!

Page protectors come in three weights: *economy, medium,* and *heavy*. Although all are safe for your photos, there is a cost difference. Economy is the cheapest, and heavy costs the most. Again, this is purely a matter of preference and budget. Although the heavy protectors look nice, they aren't essential to a good scrapbook. Buy what you can afford.

Plain and Simple

Economy, medium, and **heavy weight** are terms that refer to the different weights of page protectors available. Economy is lightweight, medium is a bit thicker, and heavy is the thickest.

Do you have a special group of pictures that you don't want to split up? Then try the latest panoramic page protectors—they spread out to show four pages at one time. Try this for your vacation photos that include your oversize photos of the cruise ship you took, along with your tickets and itinerary. These are also great to use with the before and after construction photos you took of your renovated house. Pick up a pack of these the next time you're shopping and create some great panoramic pages.

CK OK Guidelines for Plastic
(for Sheet Protectors, Enclosures, and Encapsulation)

Made of plastic: polypropylene, polyethylene, polyester (Mylar D or Melinex by DuPont)

No polyvinyl chloride (PVC), commonly known as "vinyl"

Clear, colorless

Odorless

Untreated, no coating on the side next to photograph emulsion or negative

Must not crack or break with age

Must not contain any plasticizers, surface coatings, UV inhibitors, or absorbents, and must be guaranteed to be nonyellowing with natural aging

Must pass the P.A.T. (Photo Activity Test)

Card Stock: Backbone for Your Book

Now that you have the photos, some adhesives, some pens to write about your pictures, and your page protectors, you need some paper to put everything on. Here is a rundown of basic mounting paper.

The term "mounting paper" refers to *card stock*—the usual choice for scrapbooking. Card stock works well because it is thick and heavy—sturdy enough to mount all sorts of photos and textiles. When you use lightweight paper, such as a pattern paper, as a background, it's a good idea to slip a piece of card stock into the protector so the page will be firmer.

Card stock is the backbone of scrapbooking. Because it is so sturdy, it holds everything together, and it is very affordable. Available from 8 to 25 cents a sheet, you can afford to use this paper for everything—from mounting paper to die cuts to borders.

def·i·ni·tion **Plain and Simple**

Card stock is thick, sturdy paper available in a variety of weights.

Typically, card stock is sold in solid colors, as well as marble and parchment styles. Hundreds of colors are available, so even if you can't find the perfect shade of red to match the photo of the brick on your new house, you'll be able to come pretty close!

CK OK Guidelines for Paper
(for Photo Albums, Journals, and Photocopying)

Papers that come in contact with color photographs:

pH of 6.5 to 7.5 and must not exceed 8.0

Alkaline buffered (although unbuffered is recommended)

Lignin-free, 1 percent maximum

Colorfast, no fugitive dye

Must pass the P.A.T. (Photo Activity Test)

Papers that are used with everything else:

pH of 7.0 to 9.5

Buffered with 2 percent minimum calcium carbonate, magnesium, or zinc

Lignin-free, 1 percent maximum

Colorfast, no fugitive dye

I often find great paper at a craft store, but I'm not sure whether it is acid-free. That's when I use a pH testing pen. With a small stroke of the pen, I can tell if the paper is safe to use. It turns a certain color if the paper is acidic, depending on the brand of pen you have. Another use for it is to see if memorabilia, like certificates and cards, are acid-free and safe to put in your book.

Memories to Last a Lifetime

Scrapbooking is a great family activity for many reasons. First, it is something you can do together as a family—everyone can participate. Young children can help by placing stickers, deciding between two or three colors, or sorting and ordering photos. Older children can write in captions for photos, cut and trace shapes, and help assemble pages. Even teens can get into the act with captions, themes, and collecting memorabilia.

Second, it's a great opportunity to gather everyone together and talk about important times and events in your family history.

Finally, it creates a lasting memory—both in the process and in the product—that will help to bind your family together.

You don't have to know all the terms in this chapter to get started scrapping. You can start small—maybe do one book of this year's family vacation—and see what supplies and procedures work best for your family. There are tons of resources on scrapbooking to get you going, including thematic kits that contain just about everything you need to put a book together.

A book of your family vacation is a natural place to start. It's family time condensed into a short period and usually there are photos galore. Another starting point is the beginning of a new year. Label a box for the coming year and all year long encourage family members to toss in ticket stubs, photos, notes, whatever is meaningful. Then spend New Year's Eve reminiscing and remembering the blessings God has given you as you assemble pages for a book of the past year.

Here are some other ideas that might get your creative juices flowing:

- Christian Character (build pages around values like trust, love, freedom, etc.)
- Our Family History
- School Days
- Road Trips
- Holiday Traditions
- Games We Play
- Honor Roll (awards, accomplishments, and achievements)
- Our Favorite Things (pets, food, people, etc.)

Scrapbooks can be assembled by your family to give as gifts to extended family members or friends or kept as part of your own family heritage. Preserving your family memories in this way communicates to your children that being a family is fun, lasting, and worth remembering.

Appendix A

Resources and Supplies

Books

Cook Communications Ministries. *A Gaggle of Giggles and Games*. Colorado Springs: Cook Communications Ministries, 2002.

Bell, R. C. *The Boardgame Book*. London: Marshal Cavendish Ltd., 1979.

Cambria, Phyllis, and Patty Sachs. *The Complete Idiot's Guide to Throwing a Great Party*. Indianapolis: Alpha Books, 2000.

Carlson, Dolly. *Christmas Gifts from the Heart*. Colorado Springs: Cook Communications Ministries, 2000.

Frey, Richard. *According to Hoyle*. New York: Fawcett-Columbine, 1956.

Furman, Liz. *Traditions and Recipes that Say WELCOME HOME All Year 'Round*. Colorado Springs: Cook Communications Ministries, 2003.

Klutz Press. *The Book of Classic Board Games*. Palo Alto, CA: Klutz Press, 1990.

LeBon, Marilee. *The Complete Idiot's Guide to Holiday Crafts*. Indianapolis: Alpha Books, 2002.

———. *The Complete Idiot's Guide to Making Great Gifts*. Indianapolis: Alpha Books, 2001.

———. *Have Fun with Your Kids The Lazy Way*. Indianapolis: Alpha Books, 1999.

Lockwood, Georgene. *The Complete Idiot's Guide to Crafts with Kids*. Indianapolis: Alpha Books, 1998.

Parsons, Susan, with Lois Keffer. *Funtastic Kid Crafts*. Colorado Springs: Cook Communications Ministries, 2002.

Petričić, Dušan, and Camilla Gryski. *Let's Play: Traditional Games of Childhood*. Toronto: Kid's Can Press, Ltd., 1995.

Rice, Wayne, and Mike Yaconelli. *Play It! Great Games for Groups*. Grand Rapids, MI: Zondervan Publishing House, 1986.

Smedley, Wendy. *The Complete Idiot's Guide to Scrapbooking Illustrated, Second Edition*. Indianapolis: Alpha Books, 2003.

Wall, Jeanette Ryan. *More Games and Giggles*. Middleton, WI: Pleasant Co. Publishing, 1998.

Bible-Based Board Games

Several Christian publishers have produced games that promote Bible-learning and family values. You can purchase these at your local Christian bookstore. Here are a few titles to ask for:

Bible Brainstorm (ages 9 and up)

Bible Categories Game (ages 9 and up)

Bible Challenge Board Game (ages 8 to 12)

Bible Charades (ages 10 and up)

Family Choices Board Game—Proverbs Edition

The New Kid's Choices Game

The New Teen Choices Game

Magazines

Art and Crafts
700 East State Street
Iola, WI 54900
715-445-2214

Crafts
PO Box 56010
Boulder, CO 80323
1-800-727-2387

Family Fun
commerce.cdsfulfillment.com/FAF/custserv.cgi

Online Resources

www.childfun.com

www.christiancrafters.com

www.craftideas.com

www.orientaltrading.com

www.family.com

www.familygamenight.com

www.family.go.com

www.holidays.net

www.familyplay.com

www.gameskidsplay.com

Appendix B

Glossary

acrylic paints Craft paints that clean up easily with soap and water and produce vivid, permanent colors.

anagram A word or phrase created by transposing the letters in another word or phrase. For example, anagrams of *tea* are *eat* and *ate*.

basket filler Torn, shredded, or folded material that fills the bottom of a gift basket (crepe paper, tissue paper, raffia, Spanish moss, and so on).

board games Games of strategy—such as Checkers or Monopoly—that you play by moving pieces around on a game board.

capture A move made in Checkers where one "jumps" his opponent's piece and removes it from the game board, thereby "capturing" the other side's checkers piece by piece.

card stock Special papers used for making stationery or greeting cards.

clear acrylic finish spray A clear protective spray-on finish for craft projects.

craft glue Thick, white glue that bonds quickly and dries clear.

craft paints Water-based paints that provide vivid, lasting colors (same as acrylic paints).

craft sticks Sticks that resemble Popsicle sticks, but have notches in the sides to facilitate building projects. The sticks can be inserted into each other or snapped apart at the notched sections.

crepe paper Decorative paper, similar to tissue paper, which is used in various craft projects.

crimper A tool for making shredded, uniquely shaped bits of paper that can be used in craft projects.

decorative-edge scissors   Scissors that make a decorative line on the object being cut.

doubles   Two people on a team.

endorphin   One of several morphinelike substances manufactured in our bodies to reduce stress and relieve pain. Some foods, including chocolate and chili peppers, are endorphin-producing, along with exercise, relaxation, and laughter.

Exacto knife   A sharp-blade knife used in precision cutting.

excelsior moss   A natural fiber filler for baskets or boxes.

fabric glue   An adhesive used for gluing objects to material or holding material pieces together.

fabric paint   Machine-washable paint used on fabric.

felt   Fabric made of a composite material that has no raw edges.

flocking kits   Kits that contain adhesive and fibers in squeeze bottles, for making a flocked effect on projects.

foam sheet   Flexible foam material used in craft projects to replace construction paper.

foam sheet cutouts   Shapes that are pre-cut from foam sheets.

game   Any activity used for diversion, amusement, and enjoyment.

garden stone   A painted stone (usually slate) that decorates a garden.

glass pieces (decorative)   Pieces of glass that are clear or translucent with smooth edges, which are used in mosaics, candle-making, and other projects.

glue gun   A tool that dispenses melted glue.

glue sticks   Hardened sticks of glue that are clear, colored, or glitter, which are used in a glue gun. Colored or glitter glue sticks are used to make designs on projects.

group (or set)   Three cards of the same rank (such as three 3s).

grout   A powdered material that can be mixed with water and applied to a mosaic to fill in the spaces between the decorative pieces.

high back   A term used in Leap Frog for bending over and holding one's ankles and making one's position more challenging for the leaper.

jewelry wire   Wire that comes in different gauges and colors that can be used in jewelry-making or other wire projects.

low back   A term used in Leap Frog for getting down on one's knees, tucking one's head under, and making oneself as small as possible—a good position to be in for little leapers.

magnet sheet   Sheet of magnetic material that can be cut to size and used for refrigerator magnets or other magnetic crafts.

mosaic adhesive   The glue that holds mosaic pieces in place.

mosaic sealant   A sealer that protects and fortifies a mosaic project.

mosaics   Works of art that are designed from grout and pieces of materials such as glass, stone, or tile.

paint, peel, and stick-on paints   Translucent, squeezable paints used to make designs on a plastic template (styrene blank), which can be peeled off when dry and stuck onto glass surfaces.

painter markers   Markers that are filled with acrylic paint and can be used in place of painting with a paintbrush.

papier-mâché   A French word that describes a material consisting of paper pulp mixed with glue or paste, which can be molded into various shapes when wet and becomes hard when dry.

parlor game   A game that is meant to be played indoors.

pom-poms   Cottony balls of various colors and sizes that are used in craft projects.

pony beads   Round, plastic beads that come in assorted colors and can be used in many different craft projects.

poster paints   Vivid, water-based, nonpermanent paints that are easy for children to handle.

raffia   A fibrous ribbon used in craft projects, which is made from a plant.

referee   Someone chosen as the official having final authority in administering a game. The ref makes the call when an action is questioned.

rules   A prescribed guide for conduct, telling participants how to proceed with each course of action.

run-on transfers   People and animal faces and other objects that can be rubbed onto a project with a wooden tool.

salt dough   A sculpting dough made out of flour, water, and salt that hardens when baked.

scrapbook pack   Tablets or packs of paper used in scrapbook-making that contain print designs, background, cut-outs, and patterns for enhancing a scrapbook or photo album.

sculpting clay   A pliable material that can be molded into sculptures and baked to harden.

shrink shapes   A craft medium used to paint a design on plastic. Cut out, it is baked in an oven to shrink it.

snow-texture paint   A white texture paint that comes in a jar and can be painted onto a project to resemble snow.

Spanish moss   A natural plant that is used in flower arrangements and other craft projects.

sponge painting   Painting a project using sponge shapes dipped in paint.

sponge stamps   Shapes made out of sponges that can be used to form designs with paint.

stencils   Designs cut out of plastic that can be filled in with stencil paint to create pictures on projects.

styrene blanks   Clear, plastic boards used to make designs for paint, peel, and stick-on transparent paint.

tacky glue   Clear glue used in craft projects that is thicker than white glue and stays in place when applied.

tempera paints (nontoxic)   Poster paints that are nonpoisonous and can be used when working with children.

textured paper   Fancy papers used for making cards, origami, or scrapbook packs.

tile-cutting tool   A tool that resembles a pair of pliers that can be used to cut tiles to fit into mosaic works.

white glue   Traditional school glue that is used in craft projects.

wired ribbon   Wire-edge ribbon that keeps its form when shaped into a bow.

wooden bead heads   Round wooden beads with painted-on facial features.

wooden heads (clothespins)   Rounded wooden pieces with or without painted-on facial features that fit over the end of a clothespin.

Woodsies   A trademarked product that consists of bags of wood pieces that are used to make wooden objects such as animals.

Appendix
C

Be Prepared

If you have children, you need to keep a supply of craft materials on hand. Family fun is often spontaneous, and there are always those last-minute school projects, summer vacation boredom, and rainy day blues to contend with as well.

One tip for organizing your supplies is to buy and label special bins for groupings of items you'll use together. For example, you can keep all your paints, paintbrushes, cleaners, foam trays, and so on, in one bin, and your paper goods such as construction paper, foam sheets, and copy paper in another bin. Wooden pieces such as Popsicle sticks, clothespins, craft sticks, and such, can also be kept in a separate bin or drawer; and so can yarns, threads, needles, ribbons, and so on. In other words, try to store your ingredients in groupings however it best suits you to remember where they are.

Now that you have an idea of how to organize them, let's take a look at the basic ingredients you should have on hand to become a crafting wizard. This might appear to be a long list, but you don't have to buy everything at once. Start with the most basic and age-appropriate items for your family. By waiting for after-season sales, shopping the discount bins, and giving craft kits to your children as gifts, you can easily and inexpensively put together an impressive supply of crafting materials.

The items that are in **boldface** are the most basic supplies and a good place to start if you are just beginning.

Paints, Brushes, Markers, and Finishes

- Acrylic or craft paints
- Stencil paints
- **Nontoxic tempera paints (for working with kids)**

- Special-effect paints such as crackle paint, stone finish paint, and stained-glass paints (You might want to buy these as needed for a project.)
- Fabric paints
- Textile medium
- **Assortment of different shapes and sizes of paintbrushes**
- Stencil paintbrushes and/or spouncers
- Sponges for sponge painting
- Stamps/stamp pads
- **Set of permanent magic markers** (I'd recommend ones with a thin point on one end and a thick point on the other end.)
- Basic colors of painter markers (These are optional, but they make painting small projects a snap.)
- **Clear acrylic finish spray**
- Wood stain
- Varnish
- Decoupage finish
- Paint, peel, and stick squeeze paints (These are also optional, but kids love working with this medium.)
- Plastic template for paint, peel, and stick paints

Papers and Cutting Tools

- **Pack of construction paper**
- Pack of foam sheets
- **Packs of foam-sheet cut-outs**
- **Tissue and crepe paper**
- Textured papers
- Card stock
- Copy paper
- Tracing paper
- Transfer or copy paper

- **Scissors**
- Decorative-edge scissors
- Exacto knife

Fabrics, Trims, and Sewing Aids

- Assorted colors of felt
- Material remnants
- **Trims such as lace, rickrack, and ribbon**
- **Yarn**
- Thread
- Elastic
- Cord
- Embroidery thread
- Needles
- Fabric glue
- Fusible webbing
- Iron-on transfers
- Cotton T-shirts, carryalls, aprons, and so on (to paint)
- **Feathers**
- **Pom-poms**
- **Buttons**
- Polyester fill
- Sewing machine (optional)

Glues and Other Adhesives

- **Low-heat glue gun**
- Clear and colored glue sticks
- **White and/or clear glue**

- **Tacky glue**
- Fabric glue
- Mosaic adhesive
- Spray mount

Construction Materials

- **Assorted wooden shapes**
- Wooden picture frames
- Wooden plaques
- Popsicle sticks
- **Craft sticks**
- Clothespins (spring-loaded and peg)
- Wooden candleholders
- Wooden bead heads
- Wooden knobs
- Wooden heads that fit over clothespins
- Wooden and/or cardboard boxes
- Chalkboards in wooden frames
- Clay pots (assorted sizes)
- **Sculpting clay**
- **Pipe cleaners**
- **Beads/bead wire or cord**
- Ceramic objects (to paint on)
- Glass objects (to paint on)
- Plaster
- Cement
- Decorative glass pieces and/or marbles
- **Styrofoam balls and wreaths**
- Grapevine wreaths and forms

Decorative Items

- **Dried and/or silk flowers**
- **Glitter**
- **Stickers**
- Rub-on transfers
- Flocking kits
- Foil transfers
- Spanish moss
- Basket filler

Trash to Treasure

Two good sources of craft materials that won't break your budget are items recycled from the trash bin and those collected at garage sales. You might want to make a list of the following recyclable ingredients and place it on your refrigerator to have family members save them for you. You could place a recycle bin in front of the trashcan to hold these items until you're ready to store them. You might also want to attend local garage sales to find a variety of objects that can be used in your projects. Remember, one person's junk is another person's treasure.

- Glass jars: Mason jars, jelly jars, baby-food jars
- Tin cans
- **Newspapers**
- **Foam meat trays** (disinfect and use for paint palettes)
- Foam cups
- Toilet paper and paper-towel cardboard tubes
- Buttons from discarded clothing
- Cardboard boxes
- Cookie tins
- **Sponges**
- Shopping bags

- **Paper bags**
- **Berry baskets**
- Plastic milk cartons
- Plastic soda bottles
- **Magazines**
- Cardboard boxes that hold cases of drinks (These are good to use for spraying small items with paint.)
- **Fabric scraps**

Appendix D

Quick Crafting Tips

There are so many different ways to make crafts that it's hard to keep them all straight. Here's a list of various craft mediums and the tools and materials that you'll need to accomplish a finished project.

- **Candle-making:** beeswax sheets, wax pieces, paraffin, or gel wax; candlewicks; molds; candle scent; candle dye; decorative pieces (optional)
- **Clay beads:** Sculpey or Fimo clay; plastic knife for sculpting; toothpick for making holes in the beads; cord, wire, or elastic for stringing them; jewelry closures (optional)
- **Glass-etching:** glass piece to etch, glass-etching stencils, masking tape, Popsicle stick, protective eyewear and clothing, etching solution, window cleaner
- **Homemade modeling dough:** 2 cups flour, 1 cup salt, 1 cup water, mixing bowl, rolling pin, and cookie cutters (optional)
- **Mosaics:** plastic molds; grout, plaster, or cement; decorative pieces such as tiles, marbles, or polished glass; tile-cutting tool (optional); mosaic adhesive; sponge; mosaic sealant
- **Painting on fabric:** T-shirt or other fabric product, fabric paints (I prefer the kind that come in squeeze bottles), or acrylic paints and textile medium, iron-on transfers (optional)
- **Papier-mâché:** newspapers, bowl, flour, water, acrylic paints, clear acrylic finish spray
- **Scrapbooking:** scrapbook, pages, decals, stickers, glue, markers, textured paper, decorative-edge scissors

- **Soap-making:** block of clear glycerin; soap chips; soap dye; soap molds; soap scent; decorative pieces such as herbs, flowers, or plastic pieces
- **Sponge painting:** acrylic paints, sponges with varied textures
- **Stenciling:** stencil designs, tape, stencil paint, stencil brush or spouncer

Papier-Mâché

The basic ingredients for papier-mâché are flour, water, and newspapers, but you can substitute other materials and/or fibers for the newspaper to make different effects. Follow this recipe for best results:

In a bowl, mix ¾ cup flour with ½ cup water. You could also mix about ⅓ cup white glue with 3 tablespoons water instead to make a more translucent paste.

Cover the project with the paste and add layers of torn-up strips of paper. You could use newspaper, tissue paper, crepe paper, brown paper bags, or experiment with other scrap papers. Allow this to dry until hardened (usually overnight).

The following are some ideas for projects made from this medium:

- **Papier-mâché masks:** Cover a large balloon with papier-mâché, allow it to dry, pop the balloon, and cut the ball in half. Paint the mask with paints. Feathers, sequins, and other decorative items can also be added.
- **Piñata:** Cover a large balloon with papier-mâché. Leave an opening at the knot to insert candies or treats when it's dry. Paint the piñata with acrylic paints and add features with tissue paper or foam sheets. Use smaller balloons to make Easter eggs or Thanksgiving gourds.
- **Papier-mâché school projects:** Cover balloons of different sizes with papier-mâché, allow to dry, and pop the balloons. Paint to resemble planets and moons for projects on space. One large and one small balloon can form the body of almost any animal for studies on mammals. Scrap cardboard can provide the legs.

Printing

You don't have to be an expert at calligraphy to be able to make professional-looking lettering on craft projects. These simple illustrated tips will help you make the most out of your lettering prospects. If you're really serious about doing your own printing, you might want to invest in a good calligraphy pen or marker and take a class in the art. This would be particularly helpful if you like to do scrapbooking or to design your own stationery.

Tips to making professional letters.

(Melissa LeBon)

Sculpting

You can mold various forms of sculpting materials into craft designs. Two of my favorites are store-bought and homemade types of clay or dough that you can roll and cut out or model into shapes. Projects made from both of these dough mediums can be baked in an oven to harden and make them permanent. You can paint the shapes with acrylic paints and varnish them to make a finished product.

Sculpey or Fimo Clay Beads

Make your own jewelry for your next holiday bash using this easy-to-work-with clay medium.

Knead the clay with your fingers to soften it. Roll the clay into snakes and then cut them into beads to make jewelry. Roll two or three colors of clay together to form a twisted color effect. You can also roll several colors of clay together and form a contrasting color of clay into a flat piece to cover the roll. When you cut the beads, there will be an outline color on the outside.

Be sure to make holes in the beads with a toothpick or sharp instrument before baking them. Bake the beads in a 275°F oven for about 15 to 20 minutes or until the clay is hardened. Varnish the cooled beads and allow them to dry.

This clay can also be rolled out onto a flat surface with a rolling pin and cut out with cookie cutters. These clay designs make nice ornaments, gift tags, or dough shapes for decorating craft projects (such as picture frames, wreaths, and plaques).

Homemade Clay or Dough

Save yourself a trip to the craft store and some of your own dough by making this pliable, puffy salt dough.

In a mixing bowl, combine 2 cups flour, 1 cup salt, and 1 cup water. Work out any lumps that may occur. If the mixture is too dry, add a small amount of water. If it's too wet (sticky), add more flour.

To make ornaments, roll the dough onto a floured flat surface with a rolling pin. Cut shapes out of the dough with cookie cutters and bake them on a cookie sheet in a 350°F oven for approximately 8 to 15 minutes, or until the edges are golden brown.

You could also sculpt your own shapes out of this dough and bake them as you would the cut-outs. You might need to add to the baking time depending upon the thickness of your project. If desired, paint your sculptures with acrylic paints and coat them with a layer of varnish.

You can make special holiday dough ornaments out of an aromatic apple/cinnamon concoction that has a delightful holiday smell. Simply mix 1 cup ground cinnamon, ⅔ cup applesauce, and 1 tablespoon white glue in a mixing bowl. Mix well and roll out onto a flat surface with a rolling pin. Cut out shapes with cookie cutters and bake in a 350°F oven for 8 to 15 minutes or until the dough turns golden brown on the edges.

Index

Introducing a new series from Alpha Books with a clear Christian family focus

christian family guide

Christian Family Guides are warm, conversational books jam-packed with expert content, Scripture quotes, meditations, family perspectives, and helpful resources.

Well-known Christian book author and former editorial director for Moody Press, Jim Bell Jr., serves as the *Christian Family Guide* series editor.

ISBN: 0-02-864436-0

ISBN: 0-02-864442-5

ISBN: 0-02-864443-3

Christian Family Guide to Managing People	ISBN: 0-02-864454-9
Christian Family Guide to Starting Your Own Business	ISBN: 0-02-864476-X
Christian Family Guide to Organizing Your Life	ISBN: 0-02-864493-X
Christian Family Guide to Family Activities	ISBN: 1-59257-077-1
Christian Family Guide to Family Devotions	ISBN: 1-59257-076-3
Christian Family Guide to Married Love	ISBN: 1-59257-078-X
Christian Family Guide to Surviving Divorce	ISBN: 1-59257-096-8

$15.95
Popularly priced for the cost-conscious family!